CAMBRIDGE LIBRARY COLLECTION

Books of enduring scholarly value

Spiritualism and Esoteric Knowledge

Magic, superstition, the occult sciences and esoteric knowledge appear regularly in the history of ideas alongside more established academic disciplines such as philosophy, natural history and theology. Particularly fascinating are periods of rapid scientific advances such as the Renaissance or the nineteenth century which also see a burgeoning of interest in the paranormal among the educated elite. This series provides primary texts and secondary sources for social historians and cultural anthropologists working in these areas, and all who wish for a wider understanding of the diverse intellectual and spiritual movements that formed a backdrop to the academic and political achievements of their day. It ranges from works on Babylonian and Jewish magic in the ancient world, through studies of sixteenth-century topics such as Cornelius Agrippa and the rapid spread of Rosicrucianism, to nineteenth-century publications by Sir Walter Scott and Sir Arthur Conan Doyle. Subjects include astrology, mesmerism, spiritualism, theosophy, clairvoyance, and ghost-seeing, as described both by their adherents and by sceptics.

Euphrates

This is the final book written by Thomas Vaughan (1621–66), the seventeenth-century occultist and alchemist. Originally published under Vaughan's penname, Eugenius Philalethes, in 1655, the work found a new audience in the Rosicrucian circles of the nineteenth century, when William Wynn Westcott, Supreme Magus of the Society, republished the volume in 1896 with a commentary by an associate, S.S.D.D. 'I have read many Alchemical Treatises', its annotator comments, 'but never one of less use to the practical Alchemist than this.' For its later readers, however, the value of the text lay in its insights into the history of hermetic thought rather than its alchemical advice. An important work of occultist philosophy in both its seventeenth- and nineteenth-century contexts, it purports to reveal nothing less than the origin of all life. The paragraph-by-paragraph commentary in turn demonstrates the history of its reception and interpretation.

T0352298

Cambridge University Press has long been a pioneer in the reissuing of out-of-print titles from its own backlist, producing digital reprints of books that are still sought after by scholars and students but could not be reprinted economically using traditional technology. The Cambridge Library Collection extends this activity to a wider range of books which are still of importance to researchers and professionals, either for the source material they contain, or as landmarks in the history of their academic discipline.

Drawing from the world-renowned collections in the Cambridge University Library and other partner libraries, and guided by the advice of experts in each subject area, Cambridge University Press is using state-of-the-art scanning machines in its own Printing House to capture the content of each book selected for inclusion. The files are processed to give a consistently clear, crisp image, and the books finished to the high quality standard for which the Press is recognised around the world. The latest print-on-demand technology ensures that the books will remain available indefinitely, and that orders for single or multiple copies can quickly be supplied.

The Cambridge Library Collection brings back to life books of enduring scholarly value (including out-of-copyright works originally issued by other publishers) across a wide range of disciplines in the humanities and social sciences and in science and technology.

Euphrates

Or, the Waters of the East

Thomas Vaughan
Edited by Florence Farr
and W. Wynn Westcott

CAMBRIDGE
UNIVERSITY PRESS

CAMBRIDGE UNIVERSITY PRESS

Cambridge, New York, Melbourne, Madrid, Cape Town,
Singapore, São Paolo, Delhi, Mexico City

Published in the United States of America by Cambridge University Press, New York

www.cambridge.org
Information on this title: www.cambridge.org/9781108044226

© in this compilation Cambridge University Press 2012

This edition first published 1896
This digitally printed version 2012

ISBN 978-1-108-04422-6 Paperback

Collectanea Hermetica

EDITED BY

W. WYNN WESTCOTT, M.B.,

Supreme Magus of the Rosicrucian Society.

VOLUME VII.

EUPHRATES

OR THE

WATERS OF THE EAST

By EUGENIUS PHILALETHES.

1655.

With a Commentary by

S. S. D. D.

London :

Theosophical Publishing Society
7, Duke Street, Adelphi, W.C.
Benares : Theosophical Publishing Society
Madras : "The Theosophist" Office, Adyar
1896

EDITOR'S PREFACE.

My friend S. S. D. D. has contributed a Commentary to this very curious and highly mystical tract, which was written by that eminent Rosicrucian Adept, Thomas Vaughan, and published by him under the pseudonym of Eugenius Philalethes. The seriously minded mystical student will find much to instruct and interest in the learned comments with which this edition is enriched.

The Paragraphs of the original work have been numbered for convenience of reference, and the new notes and com-ments have been placed after each numbered portion.

It must be borne in mind that there is an essential differ-ence between the meaning of the word "element" as used by Vaughan, and the modern scientific meaning of the word.

For the ancient and mediæval philosophers knew nothing of our modern theory of chemical elements; their view of the common origin of matter not recognizing such definite and independent substances.

The word "Element" as used by the learned at the period when "Euphrates" was penned, meant rather a "state" of matter, such as the hot, cold, moist and dry natures; or the solid, liquid, gaseous or ethereal conditions; or the stationary, slow, quick or instantaneous processes of change.

No alteration has been made in the text of Vaughan's work except in the mode of spelling of a few words, the omission of italics and the correction of misprints.

It is intended to issue shortly the "Lumen de Lumine" of the same author, these two volumes will be found to be mutually explanatory.

W. WYNN WESTCOTT.

EUPHRATES,

Or the Waters of the East;

Being a short Discourse of that Secret Fountain, whose Water flows from Fire; and carries in it the Beams of the Sun and Moon.

By EUGENIUS PHILALETHES

Sadith, ex. Lib. Sacro. Dixit Deus, Cujus Nomen sanctificetur: " Fecimus ex Aqua omnem Rem."

London :

Printed for Robert Boulter at the Turk's Head in Cornhill over against the Royall Exchange, 1655.

TO THE READER.

I HAVE Reader, (and I suppose it is not unknown to
thee) within these few years, in several little Tracts
delivered my Judgement of Philosophie, I say of
Philosophie, for Alchymie in the common acceptation,
and as it is a torture of Metals, I did never believe,
much less did I study it. In this print, my books
being perused will give thee evidence; for there I refer
thee to a subject that is universal, that is the foundation of all Nature, that is the matter whereof all things
are made, and wherewith being made are nourished.
This I presume can be no metal, and therefore as I
ever disclaimed Alchimie in the vulgar sense, so I
thought fit to let the Alchimists know it, least in the
perusal of my Writings they should fix a construction
to some passages, which cannot suit with the Judgement of their Author. Hence thou mayest see what
my conceptions were, when I began to write, and now
I must tell thee they are still the same, nor hath my
long experience weakened them at all, but invincibly
confirmed them. But to acquaint thee how ingenuous
I am, I freely confess, that in my practise I waved my
own principles, for having miscarried in my first
attempts, I laid aside the true subject, and was content
to follow their Noise, who will hear nothing but
Metals. What a drudge I have been in this school,
for three years together, I will not here tell thee, it
was well that I quitted it at last, and walk'd again
into that clear light, which I had foolishly forsaken. I
ever conceived that in metals there were great secrets,
provided they be first reduc'd by a proper dissolvent,

but to seek that Dissolvent, or the matter whereof it is made, in Metals, is not only Error but Madness. I have for the Truths sake, and to justify my innocent and former Discourses, added to them this little piece; which perhaps is such, and hath in it so much, as the World hath not yet seen published. It is not indeed the tenth part of what I had first design'd, but some sober Considerations made me forbear, as my sudden and abrupt Close will inform thee. However, what I now reserve, as to the Philosophical Mysteries may be imparted hereafter in our Meteorologie; and for the Theological, we shall draw them up for our own private use in our Philosophia Gratiae. I have little more to say, but if it may add anything to thy content, I can assure thee here is nothing affirm'd, but what is the fruit of my own experience. I can truly say of my own, for with much labour have I wrung it out of the Earth, nor had I any to instruct me; for I was never so fortunate as to meet with one man, who had the ability to contribute to me in this kind. I would not have thee build mountains on the Foundation I have here laid, not especially those of Gold; But if thou dost build Physick upon it, then have I hew'd thee the Rock and the Basis of that famous art, which is so much profest, and so little understood; here thou shalt find the true subject of it demonstrated, and if thou art not very dull, sufficiently discovered; Here God himself and the Word of God leads thee to it; Here the Light shews thee Light, and here hast thou that Testimony of Iamblicus, and the Aegyptian Records cleared namely, that God sometimes delivered to the ancient Priests and Prophets a certain matter, *per beata spectacula*, and communicated it for the use of Man. I shall conclude with this Admonition; if thou would'st know Nature, take heed of Antimonie and the common metalls; seek onely that very first mixture of elements, which Nature makes in the great world; seek it I say, whil'st it is fresh and new, and having found it, conceal it. As for the use of it, seek not that altogether in Books, but rather beg it at the Hands of God, for it is properly his gift, and never man attain'd to it, without a clear and sensible assistance from above ; Neglect not my Advice in this, though it may seem ridiculous to those that are overwise and have the mercies of God in derision. Many men live in this World without God ; they have no Visits from him, and therefore laugh at those that seek him, but much more at those that have found him. St. Paul gloried in his Revelations, but he that will do so now shall be number'd among Ranters and Anabaptists. But let not these things divert thee, if thou servest God, thou servest a good Master, and he will not keep back thy Wages. Farewell in Christ Jesus.

E. P.

OF THE ADDRESS TO THE READER.

By S. S. D. D.

Let no man take up this book in the hope of finding it to contain a treatise on the transmutation of metals. It is rather a very profitable study of the philosophy of nature and a guide to the attainment of that perfection of mind and body, which has been called by some, the achievement of Adeptship.

Thomas Vaughan, who wrote under the name of Eugenius Philalethes, the lover of truth, published this work in 1655. At a time when the struggles between Puritans and Catholics had reached an acute stage. At a time when it was dangerous to write openly, and when man was still supposed to be the end of Creation. Spinoza was writing his exposure of the ignorance of Bible commentators and of the vulgar interpretation of the Scriptures; Hume's famous essay on miracles was still unthought of; Nature was degraded as the enemy of God much in the same way as Woman was looked upon as the temptress of Man.

Luther's demand that the "sacred oracles" should be placed in the hands of the unlearned, while it exposed the restrictions of the Priestly teaching was still doing as much harm as good. For without much learning, the words of the Jewish scriptures may be twisted into enough contradictory dogmas to furnish the battle cries of opposing sects till the end of time.

It is impossible to understand the Old Testament while we are ignorant of the esoteric construction put upon it by the Jews; and this key to its secret meaning is given in the Qabalah. That Thomas Vaughan was a Qabalist there is no doubt; but he dared not openly acknowledge the fact; so

that we shall find him frequently speaking in a manner that
obliges him to excuse himself to the learned and acknowledge
that he writes thus " for the sake of those with weak consciences."

Our author says that he treats of a " subject which is universal;" that is to say, of a subject which has its analogies on
all planes, a subject " which is the *foundation* of all nature."

Now the Foundation was the special name used by English
Qabalists to translate the word Jesod, which is the Ninth
Sephira, or absolute emanation of the manifesting God : and
the waters of the fourth river of Eden, Phrath or Euphrates,
flow down through the foundation of life into the visible
universe.

The Egyptians, in whose secret archives we find the origin
of much of the Qabalah, considered the human principle,
or Chaibt, which they represented hieroglyphically by an
open fan, to imply the emanation known to moderns as the
odour, or the Aura, or the sympathetic or antipathetic influence of one being upon another.

In like manner we may think of the Sephira Jesod as not
only a symbol of generative force, but also of this subtle
emanation acting and reacting upon all creation ; some of the
results of which are tides, tempests, affinities, love, friend-
ship ; which is in fact the foundation alike of the relationship
of a being to its parts, and of one being to another.

This odour or aura is especially noticeable in vegetable life.
It is found that the essential oil existing in the outer cells of
the petals is the source of the perfume of a flower, the lower
surfaces containing tannin and colouring matter. Now the
first action of the Foundation of life is to emit an odorous
sphere or aura or emanation of influence. From the inter-
action of this with the Ruach or spirit, the material body is
formulated from the elements. The seed being the magnet
of attraction as we shall see expressed later on in the text of
this work.

Thomas Vaughan's next sentence confirms us in the conclusion that the ideas he associates with the word Foundation are strictly Qabalistic, "That is the matter whereof all things are made, and wherewith being made they are nourished."

Now there is no doubt that in whatever form we may take our food, whether as beef, rice, or green food, it is alike resolved by digestion and fermentation into a milky emulsion in which will be found the essential oils of the various ingredients we have eaten, and that occurs before it can in any way be said to nourish us.

Again Metals can be acted upon by ferments of an acid nature and so changed into their higher form or tincture, but without the aid of the external elementary substance they are in themselves incapable of regeneration.

Having said thus much in words intended to puzzle the untrained scholar, our author closes his introduction abruptly, advising the student to apply himself to physic, or the regeneration of his own nature rather than to the making of gold.

With a final warning against metals and an exhortation to seek only the first mixture of elements which nature makes, he closes his introduction.

I may here remark that after fermentation or putrefaction, an amount of a volatile oil far exceeding in quantity the original essential oil of a natural substance can be extracted from it by the usual processes of distillation, etc.

Fermentation in this sense was one of the most important processes known to the ancients.

We may I think gather that the essential oil and comprehend with it the perfume or aura, was the physical basis of life in the eyes of the ancients. Death, putrefaction or fermentation sets free large quantities of this essence which when treated by the wise, may effect the regeneration of a particular body. Bringing about by art in a short time what nature would have effected slowly.

EUPHRATES, ETC.

Paragraph I.

It is written in those living Oracles, which we have received, and believe, that there is an Angel of the Waters : and this seems to be spoken in a general sense, as if the Angel there mentioned had been President of all that Element. Elsewhere we find an Angel limited to a more particular Charge, as that which descended at a certain season, and stirred the Waters in the Pool of Bethesda.   Nor is it indeed anything strange that Angels should visit and move that Element, on which the Spirit of God did move in the beginning.   I cite not these places, as if they were pertinent to my purpose, or made altogether for it, though I know they make nothing against it ; but I cite them as Generals, to show that God is conversant with matter, though he be not tied to it, and this is all my design.   Notwithstanding I know, that Prince Avicen, hath numbered St. John the Evangelist among the Chymists:. And certainly if some passages in the Revelation were urged, and that no farther than

Rev. ch. xvi. v. 5.

John, ch. v. v. 4.

Gen. ch. l. v. 2.

Lib. de. An. ch. v. dict. 1.

their own sense would carry them, it would be some-
what difficult to repel his opinion. Surely I am one
that thinks very honourably of Nature, and if I avoid
such Disputes as these, it is because I would not offend
weak Consciences. For there are a people, who though
they dare not think the Majesty of God was diminished, in that he made the World, yet they dare think,
the Majesty of His Word is much vilified, if it be
applied to what he hath made. An Opinion, truly,
that carries in it a most dangerous Blasphemy ;
namely that God's Word and God's Work should be
such different things, that the one must needs disgrace
the other. I must confess I am much to seek, what
Scripture shall be applied to, and whom it
was written for if not for us, and for our
instruction ; for if they that are whole (as
our Saviour testifies) have no need of a
Phisician, then did God cause Scripture to be written,
neither for himself, nor for his Angels, but it was
written for those creatures, who having lost the first
estate, were since fallen into corruption. Now then
if scripture was written for us, it concerns us much to
know what use we shall make of it, and this we may
gather from the different conditions of Man before and
after his Fall. Before his fall, Man was a glorious Creature,
having received from God Immortality, and perfect
Knowledge ; but in and after his Fall, he exchanged
immortality for death, and knowledge for ignorance.
Now as to our redemption from this fall, we may not

Mark i.
v. 17.

(in respect of Death) expect it in this world, God
having decreed, that all men should once die; But for our
ignorance, we may and ought to put off in this life, for-
asmuch as without the Knowledge of God, no man
can be saved: for, it is both the Cause and the Earnest
of our future immortality. It remains then that our
ignorance must be put off in part, even in this life,
before we can put off our mortality; and certainly to
this end was Scripture written; namely that by it we
might attain to the knowledge of God, and return to
him from whom we were fallen. And here let no man
be angry with me, if I ask how Scripture teacheth us
to know God? Doth it only tell us there is a God,
and leave all the rest to our discretion? Doth it (that
I may speak my mind) teach us to know God by his
Works, or without his Works? If by his Works then
by Natural things, for they are his Works, and none
other, if without his Works, I desire to know what manner
of teaching that is, for I cannot yet find it. If they say
it is by Inspiration, I say too that God can teach us so,
but Scripture cannot; for certainly Scripture never inspired any man, though it came itself by inspiration. But
if it be replied, that in Scripture we have the testimonies
of men inspired, I say this Answer is beside my Question; for I speak not here of the bare Authority or
Testimony of Scripture, but I speak of that Doctrine,
by which it proves what it testifies, for with such Doctrine the Scripture abounds. Sure I am, that Moses
proves God by his Creation, and God proves himself to

Moses by Transmutation of his Rod into a Serpent, and of the serpent into a Rod. And to the Egyptians he gives more terrible Demonstrations of his Power and Sovereignty in Nature, by turning their Rivers into Blood, and the Dust of their Land into Lice, by a Murrain of Beasts, by Blains and Boils, and the death of their first-born. By the fever plague of Frogs, Locusts, Hail, Fire, Thunder, and Darkness ; all which were but great natural works, by which he proved his Godhead, as himself hath said. And the Exod. ch. vii. Aegyptians shall know that I am the Lord, v. 5. when I stretch forth my hand upon Aegypt.

When he reveals himself to Cyrus, he does it not by a simple affirmation that he is God, but he proves himself to be such by the World that he hath made.

I am the Lord (saith he) and there is none else ; there is no God besides me ; I girded thee, Isaiah xlv. though thou hast not known me, I formed the Light, and create Darkness, I make Peace, and create Evil. I the Lord do all these things. I have made the earth, and created Man upon it. I even my hands have stretched out the Heavens, and all their Host have I commanded. Let any man read those Majestic and Philosophical Expostulations between God and Job ; or in a word, let Job. ch. him read over both Testaments and he shall xxxviii., v. find, if he reads attentively, that Scripture 39, 40, 41. all the way, makes use of nature, and hath indeed discovered such natural Mysteries as are not to be found in any of the Philosophers; and this shall appear in the following Discourse. For my own part, I fear not to say, that Nature is so much the business of Scripture, that to me, the Spirit of God, in those sacred Oracles, seems not only to mind the Restitution of Man in particular, but even the Redemption of Nature in general. We must not therefore confine this Restitution to our own Species, unless we can confine corruption to it withal, which doubtless we cannot do; for it is evident that Corruption hath not onely Seiz'd upon Man, but on the World also for man's sake. If it be true then that man hath a Saviour, it is also as true, that the whole Creation hath the same; God having reconciled all things to himself in Christ Jesus. And if it be true, that we look for the Redemption of our Bodies, and a New man; It is equally true, that we look for a new Heaven, and a new Earth, wherein dwelleth righteousness; for it is not man alone, that is to be Renewed at the general Restauration, but even the world, as well as man, as it is written: Behold! I make all things New. I speak not this to disparage man, or to match any other creature with him: for I know he is principal in the Restauration, as he was in the Fall, the Corruption that succeeded in the Elements, being but a Chain, that this prisoner drags after him: but I speak this to show, that God minds the Restitution of Nature in general, and not man alone, who though he be the

Rev. ch., xxi. v. 5.

B

noblest part, yet certainly is but a small part of Nature.
Is scripture then misapplied, much less vilified, when
it is applied to the object of Salvation, namely to
Nature, for that is it, which God would save, and
redeeme from the present Deprivations, to which it is
subject : verily, when I read Scripture, I can find
nothing in it, but what concerns Nature and Natural
things : for where it mentions Regeneration, Illumination, and Grace, or any other spiritual gift, it doth it
not precisely, but in order to Nature, for what signifies
all this, but a new influence of Spirit, descending from
God to assist Nature, and to free us from those Corrup-
tions, wherewith of a long time we have been opprest ?
I suppose it will not be denied, but God is more Metaphysical, than any Scripture can be and yet in the
work of salvation, it were great impiety to separate
God and Nature, for then God would have nothing to
save nor indeed to work upon. How much more
absurd is it in the Ministry of Salvation to separate
Scripture and Nature, for to whom I beseech you doth
Scripture speak ? Nay, to whom is Salvation minis-
ter'd, if Nature be taken away ? I doubt not but man
stands in nature, not above it, and let the School-men
resolve him into what parts they please, all those parts
will be found natural, since God alone is truly Metaphysical. I would gladly learn of our Adversaries,
how they came first to know, that Nature is Corrupted ;
for if Scripture taught them this physical truth, why
may it not teach them more ? but that Scripture taught

them, is altogether undeniable; Let us fancy a Physician of such Abilities, as to state the true temperament of his patient, and wherein his Disease hath disordered it. Doth he not this to good purpose? Questionless, he doth: and to no less purpose is it in my opinion, for the spirit of God, whose patient nature is, to give us in Scripture a Character of Nature, which certainly he hath done in all points, whether we look to the past, present, or future Complexion of the World. For my own part, I have this assurance of Philosophy, that all the Mysteries of Nature consist in the knowledge of that Corruption, which is mention'd in Scripture, and which succeeded the Fall: namely to know what it is, and where it resides principally: as also to know what Substance that is, which resists it most, and rewards it, as being most free from it, for in these two consist the Advantages of life and death. To be short, Experience, and Reason grounded thereupon. I have taught me, that Philosophy and Divinity are but one, and the same science: but man hath dealt with knowledge, as he doth with Rivers, and Wells, which being drawn into several pipes are made to run several ways, and by this accident come at last to have several names. We see that God in his work, hath united spirit and matter, visibles and invisibles, and out of the union of spiritual, and natural substances riseth a perfect compound, whose very nature, and Being consists in that union. How then is it possible to demonstrate the Nature of that Compound by a divided

Theory of Spirit by itself and matter by itself? for if the nature of a Compound consists in the Composition of Spirit and matter, then must not we seek that Nature in their separation, but in their mixture and Temperature, and in their mutual mixt Actions and Passions. Besides: who hath ever seen a spirit without matter, or matter without spirit, that he should be able to give us a true Theory of both principles in their simplicity? Certainly, no man living. It is just so in Divinity, for if by evasion we confine Divinity to God in the abstract, who (say I) hath even known him so? Or, who hath received such a Theology from him, and hath not all this while delivered it unto us? Verily, if we consider God in the abstract, and as he is in himself, we can say nothing of him positively, but we may something negatively, as Dionysius hath done, that is to say, we may affirm what he is not, but we cannot affirm what he is. But if by Divinity, we understand the Doctrine of Salvation, as it is laid down in scripture, then verily it is a mixed Doctrine, involving both God and Nature. And here I doubt not to affirme That the Mystery of Salvation can never be fully understood without Philosophy, not in its just latitude, as it is an Application of God to Nature, and a Conversion of Nature to God, in which two Motions and their Means, all spiritual and natural knowledge is comprehended.

COMMENTS UPON THE FIRST PARAGRAPH.

"And I heard the Angel of the Waters say, Thou art righteous, O Lord, which art, and wast, and shalt be, because thou hast judged thus." (Rev. xiv. 5).

Here we find at once our author falling in with the " weak consciences " he expected to deal with, and for the moment taking the literal meaning of the *sacred oracles.*

" For an angel went down at a certain season into the pool and troubled the water." (St. John v. 4.)

" And the Spirit of God moved upon the face of the waters." (Gen. i. 2.)

Then he circumstantially states his opinion that God's Work does not disgrace God's Word, and his object is " to show that God is conversant with matter though he be not tied to it." It is curious to note that Professor Tyndal in his famous Belfast Address to the British Association for the Advancement of Science made an almost identical appeal to his audience saying:—

" Spirit and matter have ever been presented to us in the rudest contrast, the one as all noble, the other as all-vile. Supposing that, instead of having the foregoing antithesis of spirit and matter presented to our youthful minds, we had been taught to regard them as equally worthy and equally wonderful ; to consider them as two opposite faces of the self-same mystery. . . . . Looking at matter not as brute matter but as the living garment of God; do you not think the law of relativity might have had an outcome different from its present one. Without this total Revolution of the notions now prevalent, the Evolution hypothises must stand condemned (for what is the core, the essence of this hypothesis ? Strip it naked and you stand face to face with the notion that not the more ignoble forms of animalculæ but the human body, the human mind itself, emotion, intellect, will, and all their phenomena were once latent in a fiery cloud); but in many profoundly thoughtful minds such a revolution has already taken place. They degrade neither member of the mysterious duality referred to, but they exalt one of them from its abasement, and repeal the divorce hitherto existing between both. In substance, if not in words, their position as regards the relation of spirit and matter is; 'What God hath joined together let not man put asunder.' "

It is necessary in this place to make a slight digression on the nature of God according to the Ancients. " The Egyptians recognised a divinity only in those cases where they perceived a fixed law either of permanence or change. The Earth abides, so do the Heavens, Days, Months, Seasons; these show a regularity which was called Maāt. The Gods are called possessors of Maāt or subsisting through Maāt. Truth and Justice are but forms of Maāt applied to human action " (Renouf, Introduction to the *Papyrus of Ani*). Beyond these the Egyptians believed in the Unnameable One. He whose throne the plumes of Amen's headdress barely touch. (The Hebrew root Amen, AMN, signifies stability.)

Among the Jews, the " Jehovah " holy as He was, existed only as the manifesting deity taking form in the world of matter as the holy living creatures, the forces of heat, moisture, cold and dryness; or on another plane developing as spirit, soul, mind and matter. But the real Being of Deity was called " Ehyeh," the " I am that I am," and behind Him was the Potential Being or Ain Soph Aur. For it is written " His is the Mind, Theirs are the powers."

In the same way Brahma the Universe separated its body into two halves; *Viraj*, the spiritual, intelligent nature, and *Vach* or the manifest expression of the eternal divine Ideation. But this was not the same as the Great Brahm, or "Great Breath" breathing out for millions of years, and again breathing in for the same period, becoming alternately manifest and unmanifest. So far we have spoken of the Macrocosmic God or Macroprosopus. Of the Microprosopus; the Microcosmic God of the New Testament, He through whom we can approach the vast ideal which the human brain is too small to grasp, we need not here speak further.

I must now deal shortly with the occult meaning of the Fall. The Fall means more especially—fallen into generation or corruptibility. When Isis let loose Typhon after his imprisonment by Horus, her enraged son destroyed her royal diadem and cut off her head, but Thoth—in one sense the moon god, replaced it by a cow's head. That is to say, when in the course of cosmic evolution Primæval chaos seemed to return as ruler of night and winter, the child of the spirit moving on the waters of creation laid low the glorious mother who had borne him. She, became the Nature Goddess of the earth the symbol of fruitfulness, the sacred cow, the increaser of harvest. Henceforth the processes of change became recognised as gods or "fixed laws;" death and corruption which for a time seem like annihilation, being some of these.

Of the teaching of the Qabalah on the Fall I have only room to quote the following paragraph from S. L. Macgregor Mathers' Introduction to the *Kabalah Unveiled*.

" The first two letters of Jehovah I and H are the father and mother of Microprosopus " (or the supernal Adam) "and the H final is his bride " (or Eve). " But in these forms is expressed the equilibrium of severity and mercy. Mercy being masuline and severity feminine. Excess of Mercy is merely weakness, but Excess of Severity calls forth the evil and oppressive force which is symbolised by Leviathan. Wherefore it is said ' Behind the shoulders of the Bride, the Serpent rears his head.' Of the Bride " (the cow-headed

Isis) "not the Supernal Mother" (Isis crowned with the Royal diadem) " for she bruises the head of the Serpent."

The serpent is the centripetal force, ever seeking to penetrate paradise, and " thereby constricting the efflux of divine radiation," which is centrifugal. The Adam Qadmon's exchange of the Garden of Eden for knowledge and death, must be taken to mean the exchange of uncreated thought into differentiation and evolution, resulting finally in the creation of a material universe.

On this subject much may be learnt from the first book of the *Divine Pymander*, published in this series; in the Seventeenth book it is written :—

" Moreover the things that are made are visible, but *He is invisible;* and for *this cause he maketh them,* that *he may be visible;* and therefore he maketh them always."

So we see that the Eternal one being defined, saw a reflection of himself; and the love he bore his image emanated as a third form, the Supernal Mother who aspireth to the Wisdom which is beyond. So is the Supernal triad formed.

In like manner the Holy Triad, reflected and defined, became the throne whereon the holy deific form was seated, and the Hexagram of the Macroprosopus was reflected unto the Heart of the Microprosopus.

And in this sense are to be understood the words written on the mummy case of Panehemisis, " The heart of Man is his own God."

Around the image in the sanctuary of our hearts is the firmament and the powers, and below are the Kerubim or Living Creatures.

In his book entitled *Lumen de Lumine*, our author laments the separation that has taken place between the Elemental, Celestial, and Spiritual Sciences, for he says, these three are branches of one tree.

" Out of one universal root, the Chaos, grew all specified natures and their individuals."

I must deal shortly with the nature of Chaos as understood by the ancients, because in the present volume our author evades any definite explanation of it.

Chaos, the Abyss or " Great Deep " was personified among the Egyptians by Neïth; the only one containing all—without form or sex, giving birth to itself without fecundation. She was adored under the form of a Virgin Mother. She is the Father-Mother, the immaculate Virgin. She is called the Lady of the Sycamore, and is represented as dispersing the waters of the Tree of Life. She is the Bythos of the Gnostics, The One of the Neoplatonists, The All of the German Metaphysicians, the Anaita of Assyria.

Now from this root or chaos sprang all manifestations, divine, celestial, and elemental, and these three are one, and if separated from each other are like the dead branches cut from the parent stem.

For some pages our author dwells on the exoteric meaning of the scriptures in a manner that concerns the modern thinker very little. But we must bear in memory the intolerance and bigotry that prevailed at the period, and that twenty years later Spinoza forfeited all worldly advantages by asserting that the vulgar interpretation of the Sacred Oracles had led to much error.

However, Thomas Vaughan having paid his tribute to "weak consciences," touches us all when he says, " God minds the Restitution of Nature in general, and not of Man alone, ... who is but a small part of nature. Regeneration, Illumination and Grace, signify a new influence of Spirit. If God and Nature be one, how much more shall man and nature be one."

Emerson has said in this relation, " Indeed we are but Shadows we are not endowed with real life and all that seems most real about us is but the thinnest substance of a dream, till the heart be touched by nature. That touch creates us : then we begin to be; thereby we are beings of reality and inheritors of eternity."

We acknowledge nature to be corrupt, but by the knowledge of that corruption is to be solved the riddle of the Universe.

The union of spirit and nature gives rise to a perfect compound. The Light of wisdom united by philosophy to experiment makes the perfect artist or creative adept.

Philosophy or the passion for wisdom stimulates the intellect, as religion stimulates the emotions: these passions or expansions of the Ego carry it beyond the limits of its own being, and tend to merge it in the all being. Here the centrifugal or redeeming force is free to act, and the constrictions of matter cease. When the Passions of the Emotions and the Intellect are set free, the Experience of Elemental Nature can be judged with safety. This then is the Esoteric meaning of the " Unity with God." " I am in my father, and ye in me, and I in you." (St. John x. 14-20.) Compare again, " His is the mind, theirs are the powers " of the Chaldean Oracles. For the perfect man stands between the finest ether and the coarsest matter, and his spirit must penetrate all.

For the world, religion means, as Cardinal Newman puts it, "the knowledge of God, of His will, and of our duties towards Him." Separating Him as a formal notion from His works, cutting Him off as a branch from the Tree of Life of which He is the very root and being. Therefore to the initiated it is no blasphemy to say that such religion is a vanity and vexation of spirit.

The world holds many half evolved personalities who have to live and learn much before they can be conscious of the latent complexities of their own natures. Their hour has not yet come. But for the more fully developed,—life daily sounds undreamed of harmonies. Just as in modern music the most acute emotion is produced by subtle changes of key, so the human being in passing from one aspect to another of a highly complex existence intensifies and enriches his being with experiences, undreamed of by the undeveloped man, just as little as, by the masters of the simple harmonies of ancient music.

Our author's first paragraph ends with the clear statement that without philosophy, or the passion for wisdom, salvation cannot be understood. Again he pleads for the union of the divine, the celestial, and the natural; for he says the very nature of the highest existence is the union and synthesis of the diverse products of differentiation.

Can we not dimly comprehend from this principle how it is that each day of Brahma (or manifestation of the Universe) enriches and beautifies the night of his repose; how Nirvana becomes more and more exquisite in its subtle harmonies, as beings are prepared for it by finer and finer complexities and variations of parts.

PARAGRAPH II.

To speak then of God without Nature, is more than we can do, for we have not known him so, and to speak of Nature without God, is more than we may do, for we should rob God of his Glory, and attribute those Effects to Nature, which belong properly to God, and to the spirit of God, which works in Nature. We shall therefore use a mean form of speech, between these extremes, and this form the Scriptures have taught us, for the Prophets and Apostles, have used no other. Let not any man therefore be offended, if in this Discourse we shall use Scripture to prove Philosophy, and Philosophy to prove Divinity, for of a truth our knowledge is such, that our Divinity is not without Nature nor our Philosophy without God. Notwithstanding, I dare not think but most men will repine at this course, though I cannot think, wherefore they should, for when I joyne Scripture and Philosophy, I do but join God and Nature, an union certainly approved of by God, though it be condemned of men. But this perverse ignorance, how bold soever it be, I shall not quarrel with, for besides Scripture, I have other grounds, that have brought me very fairely, and soberly to this Discourse.

COMMENTS UPON THE SECOND PARAGRAPH.

This is a recapitulation of the general principle that God and Nature,—Scripture and Philosophy—are to be joined together and not separated from each other in our minds.

—— ——

PARAGRAPH III.

I have sojourn'd now for some years, in this great Fabric, which the fortunate call their World: and certainly I have spent my time like a Traveller, not to purchase it, but to observe it. There is scarce anything in it, but hath given me an occasion of some thoughts; but that which took me up much, and soon, was the continuall action of fire upon water. This Speculation (I know not how) surpris'd my first youth, long before I saw the University, and certainly Nature, whose pupil I was, had even then awaken'd many notions in me, which I met with afterwards, in the Platonic Philosophy. I will not forbear to write, how I had then fancied a certain practice on water, out of which, even in those childish dayes, I expected wonders : but certainly neither gold, nor silver, for I did not so much as think of them, nor of any such covetous artifice. This Consideration of my self, when I was a Child, has made me since examine Children, namely, what thoughts they had of these elements, we see about us, and I found thus much by them, that Nature in her simplicity, is much more wise, than some men are with their acquired parts, and Sophistry, of a truth I thought my self bound to prove all things, that I might attain to my lawful desires, but least you think, I have only conversed with children I shall confess, I have convers'd with children and Fools too : that is, as I interpret it, with Children and Men, for these last are not in all things, as wise as the first. A Child, I suppose, in puris Naturalibus,

Before education alters him, and ferments him, is a Subject hath not been much consider'd, for men respect him not, till he is company for them, and then indeed they spoil him. Notwithstanding I should think, by what I have read, that the natural disposition of Children, before it is corrupted with Customs and Manners, is one of these things, about which the Antient Philosophers have busyied themselves even to some curiosity. I shall not here express what I have found by my own experience, for this is a point of foresight, and a ground by which wise men have attained to a certain Knowledge of Morals, as well as Naturals.

Paragraph IV.

But to return from this Digression, to the Principles first proposed, namely Fire and Water, I shall borrow my entrane into this discourse, from my famous Country-man Rice of Chester, who speaking of this Art, delivers himself thus.

Ars hoec (saith he), de Philosophia occulta est; est de illa parte Philosophiae quae Meteora tractat; Loquitur enim, haec Ars non solum de elevatione et depressione Elementorum, sed etiam Elementatorum. Scias H O C, quia magnum secretum est.

Paragraph V.

These words, if the Mysteries they involve and relate to were distinctly laid down, would make an endless Discourse; for they contain all that Nature doth: and all that art can do. But that we may in some order, and as far as Conscience will permit, express what they signifie: We do first say, That God is the principal and sole Author of all things, who by his Word and Spirit hath form'd and manifested those things we see, and even those things which at present we cannot see. As for the matter whereof he formed

them, it being a substance pre-existent, not only to us,
but to the world itself, most men may think the knowledge of it impossible, for how shall we know a thing
that was so long before us, and which is not now extant
with us, nor ever was (in their opinion) since the
creation? To this objection, which at first sight may
seem invincible, we shall return an answer that shall
break it; for we will show how and by what means,
we came to know this matter, and not only to know it,
but after long labours to see it, handle it, and taste it.
It is evidence enough that every Individual (suppose
man himself) is made of a seed, and this seed when the
body is perfected, appears no more, for it is altered and
transformed to a body. However that self-same body
does afterwards yield a seed which is the very same in
nature with that original first seed whereof the body
was made. I presume then, that he that would know
the generation of man, needs not look back so far as
Adam to know the first seed, for if Nature still affords
the like, what needs that fruit less retrogradation? It
is even so with the world, for it was originally made of
a seed, of a seminal viscous humidity or water, but
that seed (as we have said in our Aphorisms) disap-
peared in the Creation, for the Spirit of God that
moved upon it transformed it, and made the world of it.
Howsoever that very world doth now yield and bring
forth out of its own body a secondary seed, which is the
very same in essence and substance with that primitive
general seed whereof the world was made. And if any

man shall ask what use nature makes of this general seed, and wherefore she yields it ; I answer, that it is not to make another world of it, but to maintain that world with it which is made already. For God Almighty hath so decreed that his creatures are nourished with the very same matter whereof they were formed, and in this is verified that maxim which otherwise would be most false : Ex iisdem nutrimur, ex quibus constamus.

We seek not much whence our own nutriment comes, nor that of beasts, for both provisions are obvious. But what is that which feeds Grass, Herbs, Corn and all sorts of trees with their fruits ? What is it that restores and supplies the earth, when these copious and innumerous products have for the greatest part of the year lived sucking on her breasts and almost exhausted her ? I am afraid they will speak as they think and affirm it is water, but what skilful assertors they are shall appear hereafter.

COMMENTS UPON THE FIFTH PARAGRAPH.

Thomas Vaughan begins by defining the creative deity as the formulator and manifestor of the visible world. He pictures him as an artificer working upon pre-existent substance. As I have already pointed out, this idea is that of the Jehovah of the Jews in relation to the Ehyeh and Ain Suph Aur. This latter principle must, however, be regarded by us at present as the Divine Neith or Chaos, also explained in the notes on the first paragraph. This fundamental virgin substance is only to be understood, says Vaughan, by the study of seeds.

Now if we cut open any moderate-sized seed, we shall find an outer covering, two masses of starchy matter, and a root or radicle.

In the root we have the image of the One from whom spring the many; in the two halves the positive and negative nourishing or preserving principles; and in the coat or cover the constricting force without which manifest form is impossible, but which must be overcome for growth to take place.

The seed planted in the ground becomes a sugary fœculent mass, and in the midst of putrefaction and fermentation the new living being grows and becomes manifest. The study of embryology takes us a long way towards the solution of the mystery of life. We start with the protyle or protoplasm of modern science, we trace the beginnings of a human being through stages akin to the mollusc, the fish, the reptile, and the monkey. This protyle or secondary chaos, which so much resembles the Hyle or sediment of the waters of creation is most evident to the unscientific mind in the scum of a stagnant pool.

M. Pasteur has shewn us that the air is full of microscopic life, that it can be found everywhere, from the bloom of a peach to the liver of a pig; that it can be taken thence and made to germinate in any gelatine, syrup, or glycerine basis; that the white corpuscles of blood are minute living organisms, capable of being oxygenated, and that they, like gold, become red in the process. This is no doubt a materialistic translation of our author's meaning; but the evolution of the highest is similar to the evolution of the lowest, as is taught us by the Emerald Tablet of Hermes.

All my researches lead me to consider that the great mystery of the origin of life consists almost entirely of a measure of temperature. Life is *latent* everywhere; it merely awaits the time in the cooling of a world that is appropriate to its manifestation. Let us at the same time

C

bear in mind the Qabalistic and mystical interpretation of the
" Foundation," and its connection with the emanations of the
microcosm.

Paragraph VI.

Certainly, even that which we eat ourselves, and
beasts also, proceeds all of it from the same fountain,
but before it comes to us it is altered, for animals feed
on particulars, but vegetables abstract this sperm
immediately in its heavenly universal form. Notwithstanding I would not have this so understood, as if this
seed did serve only to nourish, for many things are
made of it, and especially that subterraneous family of
minerals· and metals. For this thing is not water,
otherwise than to the sight, but a coagulable fat
humidity, or a mixture of fire, air and pure earth, overcast indeed with water, and therefore not seen of any
nor known but to few. In vegetables it oftentimes
appears, for they feed not as some think, on water, but
on this seminal viscosity that is hid in the water.
This indeed they attract at the roots, and from thence
it ascends to the branches, but sometimes it happens by
the way to break out at the bark where meeting with
cold air, it subsists and congeals to a gum. This congelation is not sudden but requires some small time, for if
you find while it is fresh it is of an exceedingly subtle
moisture, but glutinous for it will spin into strings as
small as any hair, and had it passed up to the branches,
it had been formed, in time, to a plum or cherry.

This happens to it by cold, and above ground, but in the bowels of the earth it is congealed by a sulphureous heat into metals and if the place of its congelation be pure, then into a bright metal, for this sperm is impregnated with light, and is full of the star fire, from whence all metals have their lustre. The same might be said of pearls and precious stones, this starry seed being the Mother of the all, for when it is mineralised by itself and without any faeculent mixture, then,

Vomit igniculos suos

it sheds and shoots its fires, and hath so much of heaven that if we did not know the conspiracy we should wonder how it could love the earth. Let us now in a few words resume what we have said, and the rather, because we would explain our method, for we intend to follow Raymond Lullie, who in the fifth chapter of his testament hath laid down a certain figure, which fully answers to those words we have formerly cited out of Rhaesus Cestrensis.

COMMENTS UPON THE SIXTH PARAGRAPH.

This calls attention to the fact that difference of circumstance alone congeals the prima materia into metals, vegetables, or animals. We know very well that between the lowest forms of animal and vegetable life, between the small water fungi and the hydra or amœba there is very little to choose; in fact, if we look upon the brain of an animal as corresponding to the root of a tree, we shall find extraordinary similarities even in the more complex developments of the two great kingdoms. Minerals, on the other hand, are created and formulated at such high temperatures, and are so much more durable that it is not at once obvious to us that the principle of evolution is the same.

The Arabians called the prima materia, " Halicali," from Hali—summum, and Calop—bonum; but the Latin Authors corruptly write it Sal Alkali. This summum bonum is the Catholic receptacle of spirits, it is blessed and impregnated with Light from above, and was therefore styled by Magicians—Domus Signata, plena Luminis Divinitatis.

PARAGRAPH VII.

We have already mentioned two principles, God and Nature, or God and the created world, for that third principle or chaos that was pre-existent to the world, we shall speak of no more, but in lieu of it, we shall have recourse to the secondary sperm or chaos that now is, and comes out of the visible world, for we will ground our discourse upon nothing but what is visible, and in the front of it we place the Divine Majesty who is the sole central Eternal Principle and Architect of all.

COMMENTS UPON THE SEVENTH PARAGRAPH.

Here we find our author distinctly associates his Chaos with that which is behind Kether—the first emanation of Deity; God with Chokmah or the Abba of the Kabalists; Nature with Binah or the Aima or Mother, the third emanation. Or we may put it thus; from the Chaos or Neith sprang God or the Father, and Nature or the Mother; from their union sprang the secondary Chaos or first reflected triangle. Thus completing the Hexad of the Macrocosm.

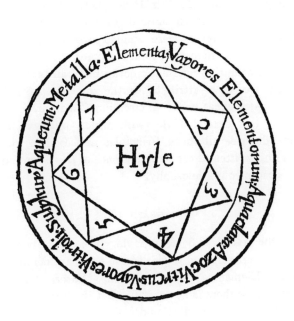

Paragraph VIII.

This Figure is Raymond Lullie's, and in the centre
of it you see the first Hyle, or matter whereof the
world was made. In this Hyle (saith Raymond) all
the Elements and all natural Principles, as well as
Means and Extremes, were mingled potentially,

in forma confusa Aquae ;

and this primitive Spermatic ocean filled all that space
which we now attribute to the air, for (saith he)

Attingebat usque ad circulum Lunarem.

Out of this central Hyle (with which we have now
done) did rise all those Principles and Bodies which
you find written in the circumference of the Figure and
here begins our Philosophy.

Paragraph IX.

In the first place over the Hyle, you see the Elements
of the visible created world, whose parts are commonly
called Elements, namely Earth, Water, Air and
Heaven, for there is no other fire but that Ignis fatuus,
which Aristotle kindled under the Moon. From the
elements on the right hand, by rarefaction and resolution of their substance, you see derived another Principle, namely Vapores Elementorum the Vapours of the
Elements or the clouds, in which vapours the inferior
and superior Natures meet and are there married, and
out of their mixture results that secondary Sperm or

Chaos Philosophical, which we look for. Next to the clouds or vapours of the elements, you will find in the figure a third Principle Aqua Clara, namely a clear water, which proceeds immediately from the clouds.

Et illa est Res (saith Lullie) argento vive vivo magis propinqua, quae quidem reperitur supra terram currens, fluens.

The fourth Principle, which Nature immediately generates by congelation out of the substance or viscosity or the Aqueous universal Mercury is the glassy Azoth, which is a certain fiery sulphureous masculine Minera ; and this is gold philosophical, the sulphor, the earth, and the Male, as the viscous Water is the Mercury and the female. The rest of the Principles which are ranged in the Figure, are artificial Principles, and cannot be known or manifested without art, excepting the seventh and last Principle, which is either gold or silver, for these are perfect metals and Ferments that specify the medicine which of itself is universal, and reduce it to a particular disposition and effect. Thus far we thought fit to deal plainly with you, and for the practice part of this Figure, we shall wave it, for we had rather speak nothing than to speak that we cannot be understood. I daresay there are some writers who rejoice in their own riddles, and take a special pleasure to multiply those difficulties which are numerous enough already. For my part I shall not put you to a trial of wit, you may take the rest from their author, and thus expose you to no other hazard, but what I have been formerly exposed to myself. We shall now again return to our theory and to make our entrance we say, that fire begins every motion, and motion begins generation. For if the Elements or parts of this material world did all of them stand in suis terminis (on their own bases) such a cessation would produce nothing. To prevent this, the Almighty God placed in the heart of the world, namely in the earth (as he did in the heart of every other creature) a fire-life which Paracelsus calls the Archaeus and Sendivow the Central Sun. This Fire, lest it should consume its own body the earth, he hath overcast with a thick, oily saltish water, which we call the sea, for sea water, (as we have tried) not to speak of its salt, is full of a sulphureous volatile fatness, which doth not quench fire like the common water, but feeds it. The like Providence we see in the bodies of animals whose heat or life is tempered with a sulphureous, saltish moisture, namely with blood, and the blood with the breath, as the sea is with wind and air. Over this Archaeus, or central fire, God hath placed in his heaven the sun and the stars, as he hath placed the head and the eyes over the heart. For between Man and the world there is no small accord, and he that knows not the one can never know the other. We may observe also, that the wind passeth between the inferior and superior Fires, that is between the central and celestial sun, and in man the breath hath all its liberty and motion between the heart and the eyes,

that is between the fire and the light that is in us. We
feel moreover in man and the world, a most even
correspondency of effects, for as the blood, even so the
sea hath a constant pulse or agitation, both spirits
stirring and working alike in their bodies. Nor ought
we to neglect another consideration, That the light of
the world is in the superior parts of it, namely in the
sun and stars, but the original fire from whence these
sparks fly upwards appears not, but lives imprisoned in
the earth, even so certainly, all the brightness of man
is in his face, for there he sheds his light at the eyes,
but the first source of it, namely that fire which is at
the heart, is no more seen than that which is in the
earth. Only this we may say, that both these imprisoned forces are manifested to reason by the same
effects, namely by the pulse, that the one causeth in the
blood and the other in the sea, to which may be added
that transpiration or evaporation of humours, which
both these spirits produce alike in their several bodies.
And that we may further prove that these terms of
Archaeus and Sol Centralis are not vain words, let us
but consider what a strong heat is required to this
sublimation of vapours and exhalations, for it is not
simple water that is driven upwards, but abundance of
salt and oil together with the water. If any man thinks
the sun can do this, I must tell him he knows not the
operations of the sun, nor for what use it serves in
nature. The sun serves only to dry up the superfluous
humidity which the night leaves behind her on the out-

side of things, for this makes all vegetables cold and flaccid, hinders their digestion and maturity. But the sun with a clear heat, taking off that extraneous moisture, forwards their concoction, and helps to ripen that which is raw. This must be done with a most gentle heat, not with such as shall make the earth to smoke and extract clouds from it, for this would not bring things to a maturity, but rather burn and calcine them. We know that if we stand long in the sun we shall grow faint, and common fire will not burn in the light of it, for the sun, which is the true element of fire, attracts it, so that by degrees it goes off and forsakes his fuel. But if you convey the fire out of the sun, then it will more strongly apply to the fuel and unite itself to it and burn it. It is just so with the earth, for while the heat of the sun is present the heat of the earth is more busy with the sun than with its own body. For as Sendevow hath well written, In superficie Terrae Radii radiis junguntur.

In the face of the earth the beams of both luminaries meet, and there is such a conspiracy between fire and fire that the central breaking forth to meet the celestial suffers a kind of extasy and doth not much mind his own body. Give me leave to speak thus, for there is such an affinity between these two, that they had rather join with one another than with any third nature, but that is it which cannot but be in part and by way of influence, God having confined the one to the centre, and the other to the circumference. I could demonstrate this sympathy by a most noble magnetism, which I have seen to my admiration, between the sun and sweet oil, or rather the fire and soul of Nitre, and here I shall tell you that the earth is full of nitre, nay I must affirm that pure earth is nothing else but Nitre, whose belly is full of wind, air and fire, and which differs no more from heaven than the root of a tree that lodgeth in the dirt, doth from the branches of it that grow in the sunshine. This attraction of fire by fire is the true cause why the heat of the earth is so weak in summer, and so strong in winter, for in the winter when the sun is absent, the central fire keeps altogether within the earth, and being irritated by an hostile invasion of cold, heats the waters much more vigorously, so that exhalations and clouds are far more copious in the winter than they are in the summer, which could not be if the sun were the cause of them. Add to this, that an outward dry heat, as that of the sun is, falling immediately on the earth, must needs burn the earth before it can make it smoke, but an inward fire, that is mingled with the moisture of the earth, cannot burn, be it never so intense, for it is qualified with the water, and tempered to a moist heat, and without doubt such a fire may very naturally resolve some parts of the earth, and cause them to exhale as our own inward heat, being moisened with the blood, makes us sweat without any violence. To reduce all this to a Corrollary we say that in the winter God seals the face of the earth with frost and cold, as a man would seal a glass, and this is to keep in the congelative Spermatic Humidity, which otherwise might ascend with the more crude vapours that break out copiously at that time and filling the sphere of the air take in, like so many sponges, the celestial vital influences. For we must know, that nature begins to impregnate the earth about the end of autumn, and continues it all winter, the fiery, subtle influx of the heavens being then condensed by the cold and moisture of the moon, who is regent all the winter and elevated above the sun. This you may see in snow, which falls in hard frost, which being taken up while it is fresh, and digested in a Blind Glass in ashes for twenty-four hours, if then you open the glass whilst the solution is warm, you shall perceive in the breath of the water all the odours of the world, and certainly far more pleasant than they are in the flowers at May. Look into the bottom of the glass and you shall find there a fat grey slime, not unlike to Castile soap, separate the phlegm from it by a soft distillation in balneo, and put the residue in a Boltshead well stopped, in a dry heat of ashes, keep it then warm for an hour or two, and suddenly the glass will fly to pieces, for the wind, the life or spirit, is not well fetled in the body. Here you may see the first attempts of nature, but if you know how to work upon the water you shall find greater things than I have told you.

COMMENTS UPON THE NINTH PARAGRAPH.

Our author calls the elements, Earth, Water, Air, and Heaven or Fiery Water.

From these by digestion and sublimation the gases, vapours, and clouds are derived. This is what in ordinary occult language is called the firmament, the Yetziratic or formative world.

From this is distilled a clear water of the nature of wine or alcohol.

By congelation is obtained a fiery sulphurous substance as wine becomes acid vinegar by exposure to a certain heat, this acetate will run into an oily burning gum or glass when duly concentrated.

Vitriol vapour and liquid sulphur are not dealt with in this volume.

I will now supply a scale of attribution and analogies between the Macrocosm and the Microcosm.

The sun and moon are allotted by Cornelius Agrippa to the eyes, as being the lights of the greater and lesser worlds.

The other planets to the nostrils, mouth, and ears.

These, then, typify the parts of the Spiritual Consciousness or divine in man.

The lungs are the seat of the firmament, and in them circulates the air we breathe.

The heart, the central fire, the Archæus. The blood with its constant pulse, the sea full of sulphurous volatile fatness.

Our author next points out that the interior heat is greatest when the light is latent.

He then says clearly that Pure Earth is Nitre, better known to us as saltpetre—a white powder which attracts moisture, and by eliminating the mineral potash forms nitric acid, one of the most corrosive acids that we have. (Of course I need not point out that another proportion of oxygen and nitrogen gives us the ordinary air we breathe. He then shows that the latent heat contained in snow will, if hermetically sealed, cause a glass to break more rapidly than the latent heat in ordinary water.

PARAGRAPH X.

The Magnesia then (as Sendivow hath written) is generated in winter, and not without reason, for then the heat of the earth is strongest, and best able to digest the nutriment that comes down from heaven, and concoct it to a viscous Sperme. But in the spring and summer seasons, when the sun hath chased off the frost, and the central and celestial luminaries have, by their mutual mixture and conflux of beams, relaxed and dilated the pores of the earth, then there is a way made for the Sperme to ascend more freely, which subliming upwards is attracted and sublimated by the vegetable Kingdom, whose immediate aliment it is.

COMMENTS ON THE TENTH PARAGRAPH.

The sap restrained by the cold of winter doubtless accumulates force proportionate to the strength of its prison walls. Like an arrow released it flies further, according to the weight of the bow which propels it.

Paragraph XI.

To return then to those first words of Rhæsus Cestrensis, we say, this Sperm is made of the vapours or clouds, and the vapours are made by elevation and depression of elements, and not only of the elements, but (as he saith) of elementates also, that is of bodies compounded of the elements, and this bears a double sense. For we must know that the earth is charged with many particular natures, as minerals of all sorts and cadaverous reliques, for our bodies also lodge in the earth when the Spirit of Life hath left them. All these, as well as the earth itself, suffer a rarefaction, and reso-lution of substance, for into these vapours, saith Raymond Lully, Omnia corpora elementata resolvan-tur ad intrandum, novam generationem [all elementary bodies are resolved, when a further new development is to take place].

This puts me in mind of an opinion I have read some-times in the Cabalists; namely that this bulk or body we have attained to by attraction and transmutation of nutriment, riseth not in the resurrection, but out of that seminal particle, which originally attracting the nutriment, did overcast itself therewith, there shall spring another new body, and this seminal particle (say they) lurketh somewhere in the bones, not in that part which moulders into dust. Of a truth we see that bones are very permanent and lasting, and this Joseph was not ignorant of, when dying in Egypt, Gen. ch. 1. he gave that charge to his brethren, Ye v. 25. shall carry up my bones from hence. We know that the Israelites were bondmen in Egypt near four hundred years after Joseph's death, yet all that time his bones were not consumed, but were carried away to the Land of Canaan, as it is written, And Moses took the bones of Joseph with him, for he had straightly sworn the Children of Israel, saying, God will surely visit you, you shall carry up my bones hence with you. Certainly if we judge rightly, we must confess that this seminal particle is our only original fundamental matter, the rest being but an accretion that comes from the extraneous substance of meat and drink. What loss is it then if we lay by this corrupt accretion or access of matter, for cannot He that made us at first of the seminal particle, make us of it again ? From this opinion St. Paul, in my judgement, abhors not, in that speech of his to the Corinthians, where he would show them the manner of the Resurrection, and with what bodies the dead rise. Thou fool (saith he) that which thou sowest, is not quickened except it die, and that which thou sowest, thou sowest not that body which shall be, but bare grain, it may chance of wheat or some other grain, but God giveth it a body as it hath pleased him, and to every seed a body which is proper for it, for so signifieth the original. And here you that are angry readers, let me be excused, for I deliver this not as my own sentiment, but as the tradition of the Jews, who were sometimes a very learned people, and knew more of the mysteries of God and nature than any other nation whatsoever. But to begin again where we left, you must know that when the central Sun sublimes the vapours, those vapours partake not only of the nature of the Earth and Water, but of divers other particular minerals whereof the earth and water are full.

COMMENTS UPON THE ELEVENTH PARAGRAPH.

Vaughan here returns to Mr. Rice, of Chester, or Rhæsus Cestrensis, whose Latin aphorism was quoted in the third paragraph, and deals with the meaning of the word elementates or secondary elements, which are generated in the same manner as simple elements by the application of a gentle heat and moisture.

Then our author is reminded of the association of the reincarnating ego with the os coccygis by the Jews; after a lengthy digression on this subject, he hints that particular minerals are to be regenerated in the same way as universal elements; we presume he wishes to point out that in the same way as simple life is generated, so a complex being can also be regenerated.

It is worthy of note that phosphorus discovered by Brand in 1669, is prepared from bones, and has many properties in common with the secret fire of the Alchemists.

Paragraph XII.

To make this more clear, the vapours properly so called, rise from the sea, and from all fresh waters. These partake of the substance and qualities of such minerals as are in the water, some of them being bituminous, some saltish, some mercurial and all of them moist and phlegmatic. On the contrary, those exhalations that come from the earth are dry, for the earth is more hot and mineral than the water. These fiery earth fumes meeting with the cold vapours of the water, oftentimes produce most terrible tempests, some of these being nitrous, some arsenical, some sulphurous and all hot, and some by reason of their copious sulphur, inflammable. Both these, I mean the earthly exhalations and the watery vapour, meet in that vast circulatory of the air, where their contrary complexions of heat and cold are mingled together like agent and patient, or sulphur and mercury, and the particular Natures and Vapours which they acquired from the minerals, are resolved by the wind, and totally reduced into general principles. It is strange to consider what a powerful resolving faculty there is in wind or air, for wind is no other thing than air stirred, and that by fire, as we feel in man, that the motion of the breath is caused by heat, as well as that of the blood, both proceeding from the same hot principle of life. So certainly the life of the world causeth wind or a commotion in the air as well as a flux in the sea, for both these are seas, and have their fluxes, as we shall prove elsewhere more fully. Air then, as we have said, resolves all things, and especially wind, for it resolves all salts into water, and if this solution be distilled, we shall find some part of the salt reduced into fresh water. As for the residue, if it be exposed to the wind, it will resolve again, and you may distil it the second time. In a word, if you repeat this process, you will bring the whole body of the salt into a volatile fresh water, nothing different from the common either in sight or taste. And here you must not think your salt is lost, for if you know how to congeal the water, you will find it again, but so altered from what it was, that you will wonder to see it. This practice, if well understood, sufficiently declares the nature of air ; but he that knows where to find congealed air, and can dissolve it by heat to a viscous water, he hath attained to something that is excellent. Much more I could say of this wonderful and spiritual element, whose penetrating, resolving faculty I have sometimes contemplated in this following and simple experiment. Common quicksilver hath a miraculous union of parts, and of all compounds is the strongest excepting gold ; for if you distil it by retort a hundred times, it will be quicksilver still notwithstanding all those reiterated rarefactions of his body. But if you take a thousand weight of it, and vapour them away but once in the open air, it will never come to quicksilver again ; for the fumes will be lifted up to the wind, where they will suffer a total dissolution, and will come down as mere rain-water. This is the very reason why also the vapours of the elements are lifted up to the middle region of the air ; for there the wind is most cold, and hath most liberty, and in no other place can their resolution, which Nature intends, be perfected. This if understood, is a most noble secret of Nature : nor was Job ignorant of it, when complaining of the decays of his own body, he delivered himself thus.

Ch. xxx.   "Thou lifteth me up to the wind, Thou
v. 22.   causeth me to ride upon it, and dissolveth my substance."

COMMENTS UPON THE TWELFTH PARAGRAPH.

Vaughan points out that the vapours of the sea are bituminous, saltish, mercurial, moist and phlegmatic. The exhalations of the earth are hot and mineral, nitrous, arsenical, sulphurous; and in the air all these things are mixed together and resolved.

He then points out that salts tend to liquefy if left in moist air. That quicksilver volatilizes, and on being divided into minute particles loses its identity in the atmosphere; but it is to be presumed that it merely turns into an oxide of mercury and falls to the earth, as many other matters do under the corrosive influence of oxygen.

Paragraph XIII.

We have hitherto shown you how fire rarefies all things, and how wind and air resolve them yet further than fire, as we have exemplified in quick-

Anima
Magica silver. And this is it we have delivered elsewhere in more envious terms, namely that Circumferences dilate, and Centres contract; That superiors dissolve, and inferiors coagulate; That we should make use of an indeterminate Agent, till we can find a determinate one. For true it is, that the mercurial dissolving faculty is in the air, and in airy things ; and the sulphureous congealing virtue is in the earth, that is to say, in some mineral natures and substances which God hath hid in the earth. Take therefore water of air, which is a great dissolvent, and ferment it with earth, and on the contrary, earth with water ; or to speak more obscurely, ferment mercury with sulphur, and sulphur with mercury. And know that this congenial faculty is much adjuvated by heat ; especially in such places where the sperm cannot exhale, and where the heat is temperate ; but if the place be open, and the heat excessive, then it dissipates. It remains now that we speak something of the two passive material elements, namely of earth and water ; for these are the bodies that suffer by fire, and whose parts are perpetually regenerated by a circular rarefaction, and condensation.

COMMENTS UPON THE THIRTEENTH PARAGRAPH.

The action of Fire tends to overcome what we call the gravitation of matter. The action of air is to transmute or oxgyenize matter. To congeal and coagulate gravitation and magnetism must be brought to bear on the substance.

Paragraph XIV.

It is the advice of the Brothers of the R. C. that those
who would be proficients in this art should study the
elements and their operation before they seek after the
tinctures of metals.   It is to be wished indeed that
men would do so, for then we should not have so many
broilers, and so few philosophers.   But here it may be
questioned, who is he that studies the elements for any
such end as to observe and imitate their operations?
For in the Universities, we study them only to attain
to a false book theory, whereof no use can be made
but quacking, disputing, and making a noise.   Verily
the doctrine of the Schoolmen hath allayed and per-
verted even that desire of knowledge which God
planted in man.   For the traditions we receive there,
coming from our superiors, carry with them the awe of
the tutor, and this breeds in us an opinion of their
certainty; so that a University man cannot in all his
lifetime, attain to so much reason and confidence as to
look beyond his lesson.   I have often wondered that
any sober spirits can think Aristotle's philosophy
perfect, when it consists in mere words without any
further effects ; for of a truth the falsity and insuffi-
ciency of a mere notional knowledge is so apparent
that no wise man will assert it.   This is best known to
the physicians, who when they have been initiated in
this whirligig, are forced at last to leave it, and to
assume new principles, if they will be such as their

profession requires they should be. Aristotle will very gravely tell us: Ubi definit Philosophus, ibi incipit Medicus; But I admire what assistance a physician can receive from this philosopher, whose science tells us: Scientia non est particularium; for without particulars a physician can do nothing. But in good earnest, did not Aristotle's science (if he had any) arise from particulars, or did it descend immediately from universals? If from universals, how came he to be acquainted with them? did he know the genus, before he knew the species, or the species before the individuals? I think not; he knew the individual first, and having observed his nature and propriety, he applied that to the whole species; or to speak sense, to all individuals of that kind: and this application made that knowledge general, which at first was particular, as being deduced from a particular object. This is true, and Aristotle will tell us so, though he give himself the lie; for elsewhere he affirms, Nihil esse in intellectu, quod non fuit prius in sensu. Which if it be true then "Scientia non est particularium" is false. But I have done with him at present, and for my own part I have learnt long ago not of Aristotle but of Roger Bacon, Quod communia pauci sunt valoris, nec proprie sequenda, nisi propter particularia. And this is evident in all practices and professions that conduce anything to the benefit of man. For Nature herself hath imprinted the Universal notions and conceptions in every soul, whether learned or unlearned, so that we need not study Universals, and this our Friar had observed; for saith he. In communibus Animi conceptionibus vulgus concordat cum sapientibus ; in particularibus vero, et propiis errat et discordat. And for this very reason, he condemns Aristotle and Galen. Quia in communibus et universalibus se occupaverunt, et perducti sunt ad senectutem, vitam consumentes in pejoribus et vulgatis, nec vias ad haec secreta magna perceperunt. Let not us do as those Hebrews did, though in this very point the greatest part of the world follows them. Let us rather follow where Nature leads ; for the having impressed these Universals in our mind, hath not done it in vain, but to the end we should apply them to outward sensible particulars, and so attain to a true experimental knowledge, which in this life is our only crown and perfection. If a man should rest in the bare theory of husbandry, and only read Virgil's Georgics, never putting his hand to the plough, I suppose this theory could not help him to his daily bread : and if we rest in the notions and names of things never touching the things themselves, we are like to produce no effects, nor to cure any diseases, without which performances philosophy is useless, and not to be numbered amongst our necessities. But how false this is, God knows and man also may know it if he considers but those two obstructions of life, sickness and poverty. But they are not only effects that are wanting to Aristotle's philosophy but even his theory is for the most part false, and where it is true, it is so slight and superficial that it doth not further us at all. He is none of our auxiliaries who believes it, but the very Remora to all natural discoveries, and he hath for many ages, not only obstructed but extinguished the Truth. Much might be said of this fellow and his ignorance, which is not more gross than perverse: I omit to speak of his Atheism and eminency of his malice, which was not only destructive to the Fane of the old Philosophers, whose books this scribbler burned, but even to the happiness and progress of posterity whom he robbed of those more ancient, more excellent and invaluable monuments.

COMMENTS UPON THE FOURTEENTH PARAGRAPH.

Study, search, think, and experiment for yourselves. So only can you find the light that will make your particular life a living reality. To accept a ready-made belief blindly is to commit mental and moral suicide. You must slay the delusions, the constrictive forces by which you find yourself surrounded when you start on your search for light. You must fight and conquer the dragons of habit and custom which stultify your spiritual consciousness; kill them and wash yourself in their blood, like the heroes of old. You must fail, and fall, and then rise again; you must strip yourself of all idolatrous shams, until you find the vivifying idea or light which shall render your life fruitful. Each man or woman must do this for him or herself. This is the teaching of the Brothers of the Rosy Cross, and it is the only living truth, for it has no finality; and the Nemesis of all reformers is finality.

But this truth has never more than half dawned upon the world ; the leader of each wave of evolution looks upon those who went before him as having erred. But the Heroic Man is always right for the time he lives in. Dante was right in the age when Catholicism was a living force ; Shakespere was right when feudalism was a living force. So Luther was right when only the husk of a religion was left, and Cromwell was in the right when the belief in the divine right of kings had died out in his race.

When we have found the constructive faith that has the inherent force to carry us onwards, we shall be right. But what that is, only the heart of each man can tell him.

In the midst of the Renaissance, through the Reformation, and Civil Wars, and after the narrowing fights of the schoolmen, Bacon called on all men to weigh and consider for themselves.

Vaughan was echoing this cry when he hurled abuse at the critic and exalted the artist and craftsman, for Aristotle must ever be the type of the former, as Plato is the type of the latter.

But we must not forget in reading the works of Vaughan, that the dawn of experimental science had scarcely appeared when they were written. For much that is a commonplace to us, would have been considered a miracle at that time ; and we must appreciate the vigour of his intellect when we find him saying so much in 1655 that is still being said by those who have thought out for themselves a complete theory of life based upon a clear knowledge of its possibilities and its limitations. Not a little of Vaughan's wisdom might be well accepted by those who study the metaphysical side of life ; but who disdain to put in practice any of the theories they are so busy in promulgating.

For, as he says, " without effect, Philosophy is useless and not to be numbered among our necessities."

Paragraph XV.

I have digressed thus far to correct this scabby sheep, who hath spoiled a numerous flock; and the rather, because of a late creeping attempt of some of his friends, who acknowledge him their Dictator, and the father of their human wisdom, and such indeed he is. But when they tell us, who write against him, that we do but restore old heresies, when indeed we oppose an atheist, and one that denied the creation of the world, and the dear immortality of our souls: they must give us leave to be a little angry with them, since we must lay the heretic at their doors, for they are the men that maintain him. In the mean time, if they are in earnest and think us guilty of any heresy, let them publicly show wherein, and we shall not fail to give them an account of our sense and their misinterpretations. For our part, we had not troubled them at this time had not one of them darkly and
T. P. timorously signified, that we teach a new physic, new philosophy, and new divinity. To whom I shall return no answer but this: that before he undertakes to judge what philosophy or divinity is new, he should first endeavour to understand the old. But this is a step out of my way, and that I may return.

Paragraph XVI.

I shall now resume my discourse on Earth and Water, and those sure are sensible substances, not Universals and chimeras, such as the Peripatetics fancy, when they couple Nature and Nothing.

Paragraph XVII.

By earth, I understand not this impure faeculent body, on which we tread, but a more simple pure element, namely, the natural central salt nitre. This salt is fixed or permanent in the fire, and it is the sulphur of Nature, by which she retains and congeals her mercury. When these two meet, I mean the pure earth and the water, then the earth thickens the water, and on the contrary, the water subtilates the earth, and from these two there riseth a third thing, not so thick as earth, not so thin as water, but of a mean, viscous complexion, and this is called mercury, which is nothing else but a composition of water and salt. For we must know, that these two are the prime materials of Nature, without which she can make no sperm or seed; nor is that all, for when the seed is made, it will never grow to a body, nor can it be resolved and disposed to a further generation, unless these two are present and also co-operate with it. This we may see all the year round by a frequent and daily experience, for when it rains, this heavenly water meets with the nitre that is in the earth, and dissolves it, and the nitre with his acrimony sharpens the water, so that this nitrous water fertilises all the seeds that are in the ground; and thus solution is the key of generation, not only in our art but in Nature also, which is the art of God. We need not speak much more of the earth, for these few words, if rightly understood, are sufficient, and carry in them a deeper sense than an ordinary reader will perceive. I know there is another Solar Oriental Earth, which is all golden and sulphurous and yet is not gold, but a base contemptible thing that costs nothing, for it may be had for the taking up. This is the earth of Aethiopia, that hath all colours in it: this is that Androdamas of Democritus, the green Duenech and Sulphur that never touched the fire, which if it be resolved, then it is our glassy Azoth, or vitriol of Venus philosophical.

COMMENTS ON THE SEVENTEENTH PARAGRAPH.

By earth our author understands nitre, salt-petre, etc. It may be suggestive to point out that in all alchemical receipts we find nitre and sea-salt (symbolised by a circle divided by a vertical or a horizontal line respectively), as the two essential constituents of the materia magica. And that aqua regia or the acid which alone can resolve gold, is made of a mixture of nitric and hydrochloric acids.

The Solar Oriental Earth is probably orpiment or some mixture of antimony, for although pure antimony is of little use in transmutation there is no doubt that it contains, under certain conditions, native properties not to be found in other substances.

Paragraph XVIII.

This is enough as to the nature of the earth, and now we will speak of the water. This element is the deferent, or Vehiculum of all influences whatsoever: for what efflux so ever it be that proceeds from the terrestrial centre, the same ascends and is carried up in her to the air. And on the contrary all that comes from Heaven descends in her to the earth, for in her belly the inferior and superior natures meet and mingle, nor can they be manifested without a singular artifice. Hence it is that whatsoever is pure in the earth, all that she receives from the water: and here I mean such pure substances as are called by the philosophers Decomposita; for the eagle leaves her egg, that is to say, the water leaves her Limosity in the earth, and this limosity is connected into nitre, and to other innumerous minerals. We have formerly told you of two suns or fires, the celestial and the central. Now both these dispense their effluxions, or influences, and they meet in the vapour of the water; for the Vulcan, or earthly sun, makes the water ascend to the region of the air, and here the water is spread under the superior fires, for she is exposed to the eye of the sun, and to the pointed ejaculations of all the fixed stars and

planets, and this in a naked, rarefied, opened body. The
air, of a truth, is that temple, where inferiors are married
to their superiors; for to this place the heavenly light
descends, and is united to the aereal oleous humidity,
which is hid in the belly of the water; this light being
hotter than the water, makes her turgid and vital, and
increaseth her seminal viscous moisture; so that she is
ready to depose her sperm or limosity, were she but
united to her proper male. But this cannot be unless
she returns to her own country, I mean the earth, for
here the collastrum, or male resides. To this purpose
she descends hither again, and immediately the male
lays hold upon her, and his fiery sulphureous substance
unites to her limosity. And here observe that this
sulphur is the father in all metallic generations, for
he gives the masculine fiery soul, and the water gives
the body, namely, the limosity or heavenly aqueous
nitre, whereof the body, by coagulation is made. We
must know, moreover, that in this sulphur there is an
impure extraneous heat, which gnaws and corrodes
this watery Venus, endeavouring to turn her to an impure
sulphur, such as his own body is; but this cannot be,
because of the heavenly seed or light hid in the aqueous
nitre, which will permit no such thing, for as soon as
the sulphureous terrestrial heat begins to work, so soon
it awakes and stirs up the heavenly light, which, being
now fortified with the masculine tincture, or pure fire
of the sulphur, begins to work on its own body, namely,
on the aqueous nitre, and separates from it, the feculent

extraneous parts of the sulphur, and so remains by
itself a bright celestial metalline body. Observe then,
that the tincture or soul of the sulphur cannot be
regenerated in its own impure body, but it must forsake
that dark and earthy carcase, and put on a new purified
body before it can be united to the light of Heaven.
This new body springs out of the water, for the water
brought it down from Heaven, and certainly by water
and spirit we must be all regenerated; which made
some learned divines affirm that the element of water
was not cured, but only that of the earth. Nor can
I here omit the doctrine of St. John, who makes the
water one of those three witnesses which attest God
here on earth. And much to this purpose is that
speech of St. Paul: How that God in times past
suffered all nations to walk in their own ways, but
nevertheless (saith he), he left not himself without a
witness, inasmuch as he gave them rain from Heaven,
etc.

The benedictions or blessings that descend from God,
are not a form of words, like the benedictions of men;
they are all spirit and essence, and their Deferents are
natural visible substances, and these are the
Gen.   blessings which the Patriarch wished to his
son: "God give thee of the dew of Heaven
from above, and of the fatness of the earth from
beneath." He was not ignorant of those blessings,
which the God of Nature had enclosed in those natural
things; and therefore He saith in the same place:

" The smell of my son is like the smell of a field, which
the Lord hath blessed." And St. Paul in his epistle to
the Hebrews tells us : " That the earth, which drinketh
in the rain, that cometh oft upon it, receiveth blessing
from God : but that which beareth thorns and briars is
rejected and nigh unto cursing, whose end is to be
burnt."

COMMENTS UPON THE EIGHTEENTH PARAGRAPH.

The whole of this paragraph is worthy of the most attentive
study, and may be interpreted on all planes, with advantage
to the student of occultism. Taking for instance the

	Natural.	*Philosophical.*	*Religious*
Passion (expansion)	Fire	The flash of an idea	Enthusiasm,impulse
Intuition (instinct)	Water	Creative imagination (Nourishing the idea)	Aspiration
Vehicle (the medium)	Air	Formulative intelligence (The word)	Emotional energy
The nourisher (the manifestor)	Earth	The completed work	Complete communion

The three alchemical principles may be taken as the
principles of centrifugal, centripetal and circulatory motion ;
or as corroding, penetrating, and preserving, according to
the commonly understood characteristics of sulphur, mercury
and salt.

E

Paragraph XIX.

But to explain what this blessing is, we remember
we have written elsewhere, that water is of
Anthrop. a double complexion, circumferential and
central. In the circumference she is crude,
volatile and phlegmatic; but in the centre she is better
concocted, viscous, aereal, and fiery. This central part
is soft and saltish, outwardly white and lunar, but in-
wardly red and solar, nor can it be well extracted
without a lunar or solar magnet, whose proper element
it is, and with which it has a wonderful sympathy.
Hence that obscure saying of the philosophers, who
when they describe unto us their mercury, give it this
character as most natural, Quod adhaeret corporibus.
That it adheres to the bodies or metals. And as
Pythagoras saith in the Turba, Suum absque igne con-
sequitur socium. And therefore it is written in the
same book, Magna est propinquitas inter magnesiam
et ferrum. We see indeed by a vulgar experience, that
if any ordinary stone stands long but in common water
there sticks to it a certain limosity, which the water
deposeth. But notwithstanding all this, and all they
say, we must needs affirm, that even their mercury
adheres not to the vulgar metals; and in this word
mercury, as in all other terms, they are not a little
ambiguous and subtle. There is indeed a mystery of
theirs in water, and a knotty one, with which many

learned men have been gravelled; and now since we have mentioned it, we care not much if we speak soberly of it.

Paragraph XX.

There is nothing so frequent, and indeed nothing so considerable in their books as fire and water, but the reciprocal and confused use of both terms, puzzles much, as when they tell us that their water is their fire. Of this they have written so strangely, that I have sometimes been angry with them; but amongst them all, I found one had a good will to satisfy me. This author confessed he miscarried two hundred times, notwithstanding his knowledge of the true matter, and this because he did not know the fire or agent by which the matter is altered. These misfortunes of his own moved him it seems, to a commiseration of posterity; but I must needs affirm he hath taken his liberty, and expressed his own mind after his own way. "Our fire (saith he) is mineral, equal, continual; it vapours not unless the heat be too great; it participates of sulphur; it dissolves, calcines, and congeals all; it is artificial to find, and not chargeable, and it is taken elsewhere than from the matter." To all this he adds that at last, whereof he would have us take notice. "This fire (saith he) is not altered or transmuted with the matter." He thought certainly he had spoken enough, and truly so he hath but it is to such as know it already.

COMMENTS UPON THE TWENTIETH PARAGRAPH.

Deals with the nature of philosophical fire, that it is moist and invisible as the heat of a hot-bed or forcing-house; or a humid, tepid fire, blood warm.

There are different degrees of heat for the black, white, and red stages of the work, but the first must be gentle and moist. Here again we have the symbolism of thought and gentle melancholy, purity, and finally practical power.

PARAGRAPH XXI.

For my own part I have found a certain mineral stinking water, which partakes of the nature of sulphur, and whose preparation is artificial, which is not of the essential parts of the matter, but accidental and extraneous, which vapours not unless it be overheated, which dissolves, calcines, and congeals all, but is not congealed; for it is expelled at last by the fire of nature, and goes off in windy fumes. This menstruous sulphureous fire against nature hath taught me how natural our work is; for it doth that here, which common water doth in the great world. In this respect it is called of some philosophers phlegma, ros, aqua nubium; not certainly that it is such, and therefore let us not deceive ourselves with misconstructions. He that would know the reason of those terms, let him take this account from a most learned philosopher. Aqua Nubium vocatur (saith he) quia distillata, est

velus ros Maii, tenuissimarum partium. Est quoque
eadem aqua acetum acerrimum, quod corpus fecit
merum spiritum. Ut enim acetum diversarum quali-
tatum est, nempe ut in profundum penetret, et astrin-
gat, sit haec aqua solvit, et coagulat, non autem
coagulatur, quia non est de subjecto proprio. Thus
much as to the terms, and now let us return to the
thing itself. I said this fire effects that in the glass
which common water doth in the great world; for as
this phlegmatic element coagulates not, nor is it at all
diminished, notwithstanding that infinite number of
individuals which Nature still produceth, even so it is
so in our work; for our water also alters not, though
the matter be altered in her belly, and our very principles generated there, namely, sulphur and mercury
philosophical. Nor should any man wonder that I
affirm common water to be incoagulable by heat at
least, for in this I speak not unadvisedly. I know
there are in water some natures coagulable, but they
are not parts of the water, but are other elements; nor
will I deny but some phlegm, nay, a very great quantity, and sometimes all, may be retained by mixture
with other natures, and seem to be coagulated into
stones, and those sometimes transparent; but coagulation in this sense, namely, by mixture of parts, as in
meal and water, I mind not; but by coagulation I
understand a transmutation of the substance of mere
water into earth or air, and this in simple water cannot
be. I know there is a water, that of itself, without all

extraneous additions will coagulate in a soft heat to a
fusible salt more precious than gold ; but this is not any
water that the eye sees, but another invisible humidity,
which is indeed everywhere, sed non videtur (saith
Sendivow) donec artifici placeat. This might satisfy
as to this point, but I will add something more, lest
I speak without reason, especially to those, who are
not willing to allow others a better judgments than
they have themselves.

COMMENTS UPON THE TWENTY-FIRST PARAGRAPH.

Deals with the putrefying agent as a centrifugal energy,
for until the elements have fallen out among themselves the
celestial influence cannot descend.

Until we are conscious of our present imperfections, we
cannot receive the perfecting influence.

PARAGRAPH XXII.

The commerce that is maintained between Heaven
and earth by the ascent and volatility of water may
sufficiently inform us of what dangerous consequence,
the coagulation of this element would be. It is im-
probable then that the wise god of Nature should make
that humidity coagulable, whose very use and office
requires it should be otherwise; for if in the essence
of water, as it is simple water, there were an astrin-

gent congealing faculty, it would by degrees attain to a total fixation, and then there could be no further generation, either of sperms or bodies; reason for it is this, if the water were fixed there would be no vapour or cloud, and there being no vapour there could be no sperm, for the elements cannot meet to make the sperm but in a vapour. For example, the earth cannot ascend, unless the water be first rarefied, for in the belly of the water is the earth carried up: and if the earth ascends not, having put off her gross body and being subtilated and purged with the water, then will not the air incorporate with it, for the moisture of the water introduceth the air into the rarefied and dissolved earth. And here again as the water reconciled the air to the earth, so doth the air reconcile the water to the fire, as if it would requite one courtesy with another; for the air with its unctuosity and fatness introduceth the fire unto the water, the fire following the air, and sticking to it as to its fuel and element. It remains now, that we observe, that the vapour of the water was the locus or matrix, wherein the other three elements did meet, and without which they had never come together; for this vapour was the deferend that carried up the pure virgin earth to be married to the sun and the moon, and now again she brings her down in her belly impregnated with the milk of the one and the blood of the other, namely, with air and fire, which principles are predominant in those two superior luminaries. But some wise ones, they argue and tell me, that this vapour being thus impregnated may now be coagulated, and fixed, by help of those hot principles of air and fire. To this I answer that the viscous seminal part of the water may, but the phlegm never, and I will show as much by example. When this vapour is fully impregnated it stays no longer in that region, but returns presently to the earth from which it ascended. But how doth it return? But Lumen de certainly not in a violent stormy precipita-lumine. tion like rain, but as I have written else-where, it steals down invisibly and silently; even if it be a vapour, such as I speak of, In quo est imaginatum semen astrale certi ponderis, then it is neither heard of nor seen till a long time after. But to proceed in what I have promised to do, I shall instance in common dew: for dew hath in it some small dose of the star fire. We see therefore that this humidity comes down silently, for its enclosed fire keeps it rarefied in the form of air, and will not suffer it to condense to water at that height as the vapour of rain doth, but when it is descended near the earth it mingles with other crude vapours, and borrowing from them a great quantity of phlegm settles at last into drops. But before we go any further let us here consider those words of the son of Sirach. "Look (saith he) on all the works of the Most High, and there are two and two, one against the other." In this he agrees with that little fragment which goes under the name of Moses, where God teacheth him thus.

Scias, quod unicuique Creaturae, et compar, et contrarium creavi. I will not peremptorily affirm that Moses is the author of this piece, or that God taught him in those very words, but I affirm that those words express the truth of God, and point at some great mysteries of His wisdom. Nor will I here omit a circumstance, namely, that this piece hath in it some Hebrew words, and this proves that the author was a Jew if not Moses. But to pass by the author and come to the sense; I say that God created water to oppose it to the earth, and this appears by their different complexions and qualities; for the earth is gross and solid, the water, subtil and fluid; and the earth hath in her the coagulating, astringent power, as the water hath partly in it the softening dissolving faculty. The earth then shuts up herself and in herself the fire so that there can be no generation or vegetation, unless the earth be opened, that the fire may be at liberty to work. This we may see in a grain of corn, where the astringent earthly faculty hath bound up all the other elements, and terminated them to a dry compacted body. Now this body, as long as it is dry, or as Our Saviour saith, as long as it abideth alone; that is to say as long as it is without water, so long it can bear no fruit; but if it falls into the ground and dies, that is to say, if it be dissolved there by the humidity of Heaven (for death is but dissolution) then it will bring forth much fruit, as Our Saviour testifieth. It is the water then that dissolves, and life followeth the dissolution; for no sooner is the body opened, but the spirit stirs in it, perceiving in the dissolvent or dewy water, another spirit, to which he desires to be united. This spirit is the air enclosed in the dew or water, which air is called in the philosopher's books Aqua maris nostri, aqua vitae manus non madefaciens. But who will believe that there is a dry water hid in the moist? certainly few: and this Sendivow tells us of some Sophisters of his acquaintance. Non credebant aquam esse in mari nostro, et tamen philosophi videri volebant. I have myself known many such philosophers, and of whom I say the very same. But to return to our business; it is called aqua vitae, because this air involves in itself a fire, which is life Universal: not yet specified, and therefore it agrees with all particular lives, and is amicable to all kinds of creatures.

Now the particular specified fire, or life of the grain, which is the vegetable magnet, attracts to himself the universal fire or life, which is hid in the water, and with the fire he attracts the air which is the vestiment or body of the fire, called by the Platonics, currus Anima, and sometimes Nimbus ignis descendentis. Here then is the ground upon which the whole mystery of natural augmentation and multiplication is built; for the body of the grain of corn is augmented with the aliment of air, not simple but decomponded, which air is carried in the water, and is a kind of volatile sweet salt; but the fire or life of the grain, is fortified with the universal fire, and this fire is involved in the air, as

the air is in the water. And here we may observe that
it is not water only that conduces to the generation or
regeneration of things, but water and fire; that is
water and spirit, or water that hath life in it and
this, if rightly understood, is a great manuduction to
divinity.

COMMENTS UPON THE TWENTY-SECOND PARAGRAPH.

It is not the vehicle that coagulates, but the matter
borne in the vehicle. Here it will be well to remember the
Qabalistic definitions of the parts of the Soul. The Earth
or The Nephesh is the aura or lower astral. The Water or
The Neshamah is the throne of the spirit. The Fire or The
Chiah, and Neshamah form the Wheels and the Throne of the
Incarnating Ego (Yechidah) or the real spirit of the Triple
Fire. While the air, or the human Ego, is the meeting place
of the other forces.

PARAGRAPH XXIII.

To conclude, the sum of all we would say is this, the
roots and seeds of all vegetables are traced in the
earth, in the midst of this dewy fountain, as a lamp is
placed in the midst of oil; and the fire or life of the
seeds attracts to itself the abryssach or leffa, I mean
the juice or gum of the water, as the fire of a lamp
attracts the oil that is round about it. Now when all
the air is drawn out of the water then the traction

ceaseth, and concoction or transmutation begins, but if
the crude water, which was the vehiculum of the air
stays with the seeds, then it hinders concoction, and
therefore the sun and the archeus jointly expel her, so
that she takes wing and returns to the region of the
air, where again she fills her belly with that starry
milk, and then descends as before. This is the reason
why there is in nature such a vicissitude of showers
and sunshine, for the showers bring down the aereal
nutriment, and when the plants have attracted it, then
the sunshine calls up the crude water, which otherwise
would hinder digestion and coagulation. This then is
the trade that common water drives, but if she could be
coagulated, this trade would cease, and all life would
cease with it. I have for many years looked upon
her as on a bird that flies to her nest, and from it
again, feeding her young ones, and fetching food for
them. Now is this a new fancy of mine, for some
learned men considered as much before; in which
respect that milky moisture which is found in her
crystal breasts is called by some of them Lac vola-
tilium, the milk of birds, and they have left it written,
that birds do bring their stone unto them.

PARAGRAPH XXIV.

To make an end, observe that there is a great differ-
ence between this common water, and our chymical
ater or fire, mentioned formerly out of Pontanus, for

our water helps coagulation and this hinders it. For
if the phlegm, or crude spirit stays with the air, the air
will never congeal; and therefore said Sendivow,
omnis aqua congelatur calido, si est sine spiritu, and
thus have I demonstrated my position, namely that
common water is not congealable.

Paragraph XXV.

Nothing now remains, not is there anything hinders,
but that we may safely and infallibly conclude, that
simple crude water feeds nothing; but the gum of
congealable part of it feeds all things; for this is the
astral balsam and the elemental, radical humidity,
which being compounded of inferiors and superiors, is
a restorative both of spirits and bodies. This is the
general vital element which God Himself provides for
all His creatures, and which is yearly produced and
manifested in the elements, by the invisible operation
of his spirit, that works all in all. This hath in it the
whole anatomy of Heaven and earth, whose belly is
full of light and life, and when it enters into these
lower parts of the world, it overcasts them with a
certain virility, makes them break forth into flowers,
and presents us with something that is very like to the
paradise we have lost. In a word this is no human
confection, but a thing prepared by the Divine Spirit;

nor is it made for vegetables only, but for man also, whom God did sometimes feed with it. This the Scripture tells us, whose authority is above Aristotle and Galen; for thus I read in Exod. "And Chap. xvi. 13, 14, 15. it came to pass that at even, the quails came up and covered the camp, and in the morning the dew lay round about the host. And when the dew that lay was gone up, behold upon the face of the wilderness there lay around small thing, as small as the hoar frost on the ground, and when the children of Israel saw it, they said one to another, it is manna; for they wist not what it was, and Moses said unto them 'this is the bread which the Lord hath given you to eat.'" Every child knows that dew settles into round drops; and here Moses tells us that when the phlegmatic humidity was gone up, the congelative part that stayed behind, was a round small thing, for it retained still the figure of the drop, in whose belly it was hid. This coagulative part is oleous and fusible, and with this also the Scripture accords, telling us, that when the sun waxed hot, it melted. It is with all of a most facile quick alteration, and therefore easily transmutable or convertible into any form; and for this reason Moses charged the people to leave none of it till the morning; but some of them (saith the text) left of it till the morning, and it bred worms and stank; whence we may gather, that it is in some degree animal. We feel then that the Spirit of God is still busy with water, and to this hour moves not only upon

it but in it, nor do I doubt but this is the ground of
that deep question, which amongst many others God
proposed to Job. "Hath the rain a father,
Chap.xxxviii. or who hath begotten the drops of dew?" it
v. 28. is worth our observation that the children
of Israel, when they saw this thing (though
they knew it not) said one to another: it is Manna; for
what argues this, but that Manna (as the words im-
ports) was some secret gift of God, which they knew
not, but had formerly heard of by tradition from their
fathers; and perhaps by such a description as Hermes
gives it in the Zaradi, namely, that it ascends from the
earth to Heaven and descends again from Heaven to
the earth; and this might make them call it Manna,
because it descended with the dew. I question not
but Moses knew it well, though the common people
wist not what it was; for the golden calf could not be
burned to powder with common fire, but with the fire
of the altar, which was not that of the kitchen. This
is plain out of the Machabees, where it is written, that
this fire was hid in a pit, and that for many years it
was there kept safe during the captivity. But who is
so mad as to hide common fire in a pit, and to expect
he shall find it there many years after? is it not the
best course to quench it, and rather drown it in a well
than bury it in a pit. We doubt not for our part, but
this fire was far different from the common, and this
the text also tells us, for when it was brought out of
the pit it was not fire, but a thick water. The truth

is that this mystery belonged to the Jewish
Magia   Church : the priests and prophets having
Adamioa   received it from the patriarchs, I mean
from Abraham, Isaac and Jacob, and
they from Noah, and all of them from Adam, as we
have proved elsewhere. These indeed were the men
that planted the world, and instructed posterity : and
these and none other must be those ancient and first
philosophers, whom Zadith calls Avos Mundi, some of
whose terms are cited by him.

COMMENTS UPON THE TWENTY-FIFTH PARAGRAPH.

But the gum or jelly of water feeds all things. Manna is a
translation of the Hebrew word Man, meaning occultly the
mixture of the upper and lower waters; the waters of creation in the chariot of the waters of the floods.

The fire that was hid in the pit, the fire of the altar, may,
of course, have been any inflammable spirit or oil, such as
spirits of wine, petroleum or a preparation of phosphorus,
limelight or even an application of electrical force. But
there is a deeper meaning to be looked for in the passage
quoted from Maccabees.

This paragraph ends with an apology for the Jews, whom,
it must remembered, were at this time, still looked upon with
loathing by the Christians.

PARAGRAPH XXVI.

We shall now (before we make an end) repeat all we
have said and that in a few words, such as shall be

agreeable to Nature and to the parts of the world as they have been manifested to us by experience.

We have certainly found, that there is nothing above but the very same is also here beneath, but in a more gross material complexion; for God hath ordained, that the gross and corpulent sperm of inferiors, should afford a body to the animating and subtle influx of their superiors. Now God hath decreed no union of sperms but of such as proceed from bodies that are of the same nature and kind, for his own word bears him witness that he hates confusion or a mixture of seeds that are different or of a diverse kind. Not unadvisably then did the priests, or (as Proclus tells us, the founders of the ancient priesthood affirm, Coelum esse in Terra sed modo Terrestri, et Terram esse in Coelo sed modo Coelesti; for otherwise they could not be of a kind. We say therefore, that in this universe, there are four luminaries, whereof two are coelestial and two are central. The celestial are the sun and moon, and they are known to all the world; the central indeed are not known, and therefore not believed, for the one is overcast with earth, and the other with water. In the centre then of the earth, there is hid a fire, which is of Nature solar, but more gross than that which is in the sun; and in the belly of the water, there is carried a viscous gross air, of a menstrous lunar nature, but not so bright and subtle as that which is in the moon. To be short, the central sun casts into the belly of the

Levit. xix. 7, 19.

F

water a masculine hot salt; and the water receiving it, adds to it her seminal feminine limosity, and carries it upon her wings into the region of the air. Thus we see how the material part of the seed is made, and now to this body of it the heaven gives life, the moon giving it spirit, and the sun giving it soul; and thus are the four lunaries brought together, the superior contributing that to the seed, which is subtle and vital; and the inferior that which is corpulent and material. This seed is carried invisibly in the belly of the wind, and it is manifested in water, I say in water as clear as crystal, and out of water it must be drawn, for there is not under heaven, any other body where it may be found. I have sought it myself in the common metals, in quicksilver, in antimone, and in regulus of antimony also in regulus of Mars, Venus, and Saturn, and of all the bodies; but I lost my labour, for I sought it where it was not. All these errors did I run into after I had known true matter; for having mis-carried in my first attempts upon it, I left it as a thing untractable; and this tergiversation of mine, brought me many inconveniences. I conceived indeed, that a vitriol made of those four imperfect bodies, antimony, lead and copper might be that glassy Azoth of Lullie, whose spirit or water, he has so magnified in his testament.

COMMENTS UPON THE TWENTY-SIXTH
PARAGRAPH.

We now come to the connecting link between the parts of this volume. We have here a series of actual quotations from the Emerald Tablet of Chiram Trismegistus, or as he is commonly called, Hermes.

Of the four luminaries I may here quote a passage from our author's book called *Lumen de Lumine*.

" ' It is most certain that no Astrabolism takes place without some grievous corruption and alteration in the Patient, for Nature works not but in loose moyst discomposed Elements. When the Elements fall out among themselves, the Celestial Fire reconciles them and generates some new Form, seeing the old one could consist no longer. . . . The body must be reduced to sperm, which receives the Impress of the Stars, and must immediately be exposed to the fire of Nature.' . . . When she had thus said she took out two Miraculous Medals. I did not conceive there was in Nature such glorious substances, she called them the Saphirics of the Sun and Moon."

The sun and the moon are the Cœlestial luminaries, but the central ones are a fire hidden in the earth or nitre, and an airy lunar nature in the water.

These two mixed natures are known to us as the desires of the flesh and the phantasies of the imagination: in their transmutation by consecration of the desires and purification of the thoughts, lies the pathway to wisdom.

The will and the imagination of an adept are symbolised by the Urim and Thummim of the High Priest; with this key read the paragraph carefully, and it will give you food for much profitable reflection.

84

Paragraph XXVII.

This indeed clinks finely, and may so swell a young
head as to make him turn poet, and like the Delphic
devil, tell a lie in heroics. No less obstructive to me
was that speech of Parmenides, in the Turba. " Aes
aut plumbum, pro pinguedine vel nigredine, et stannum
pro liquefactione sumite." What can this signify at
first sight but Antimony ? and what can this stannum,
that comes from it by liquefaction be, but Regulus.

This made me labour for a long time on this feculent
and unprofitable body, supposing of a truth, that Regulus
of antimony was white lead or tin philosophical. But
that we be not deceived, all these parables relate to
another mineral, and not to common antimony,
which the Turba condemns in these words.

Camba in Notandum est quod invidi lapidem anti-
Turba. monium nuncupârunt. Note (saith Cambar)
or observe that the envious call the
stone antimony. But what the envious call it,
that certainly it is not and Basil Valentine in his
Currus Triumphalis, which he hath written in the
praise of antimony, tells us: non tantum illi a Deo
concessum est ut in, vel ex Antimonio inventatur
Mercurius philosophicus, primum Ens, Argentum
vivum, et aqua prima metallorum perfectorum, ex qua
sit magnus lapis antiquorum philosophorum, sed hoc
primum Ens in Alio Minerali invenitur, in quo metal-
lica ratione operatio altior est, quam stibii. And the

same Basil a little afterwards, speaking of Stella martis, delivers himself thus: Plerique putarunt hanc stellam esse materiam veram lapidis philosophorum, cogitantes se veraciter hoc imaginari, quia natura stellam hanc sponte sua formavit; Ego vero nego; hi viri, Regia via relicta, per avias rapes, ubi Ibices habitant, et prædatrices Aves nidificant, iter instituunt; non id debetur huic stellæ, ut materia sit lapidis nobilissimi, licet in eo latet medicina optima. It remains then, reader that, we lay aside all common metals, as gold, silver, copper, iron, tin, lead, antimony and quicksilver. For if we seek the sperm in any of these, we shall never find it, because we seek it in metallis vulgi, in quibus non est, as Sendivow hath told us. We must therefore seek another body, which is not common, nor is it made by mixture or otherwise, of any metal that is common; but is a certain black sulphur made by nature, and which never touched the fire. This is that body whereof Albertus Magnus has thus written: Datur in Rerum natura corpus metallicum quoddam, facilis solutionis, facilisque putrefactionis, si praeparationem ejus nosti, felix Medicus eris. And after him, his disciple Thomas Aquinas speaking of the same minera, cites these notable words out of another philosopher; est quaedam species metalli, quam gens nunquam invenit. This is the metal we must seek for and it is hard to find, because we must not dig to come at it, for if we know where it is, we need no more but stoop and take it up gratis. Yet it is neither Glauber's antimony, nor

common lead, nor is it a flintstone, not the marle of
Peter Faber, who after he had wearied himself, and
deceived his readers with discourses of antimony, and
sublimate with salts of common metals, sulphur at last
in this Clod, or Marga as he calls it. But to pass by
these fooleries and come to a conclusion : I say that
this black sulphur is the male, which being found, we
are in the next place to seek the female; and here
observe, that God Almighty hath in particular bodies
made no differences of sexes, but only in the animal
kingdom, for in vegetables and minerals there is no
such thing. We see that in grains of corn (suppose of
wheat) there is no division into males and females, for
the truth is they are all males, and God hath allowed
them no female but the universal one, namely water,
whose viscous general seed joining with the particular
seed and spirit that is in the grain, is therewith fer-
mented and congealed into the same nature with the
grain itself, and so propagates and multiplies corn :
even so it is in metals, for every one of them is masculine, sulphureous, choleric, nor hath God ordained that
any of them should propagate and multiply the other
either naturally or artificially though we deny not but
that they may be multiplied by help of that seed,
wherein God hath placed the blessing of multiplication.
In metals then, there is no distinction or differences of
sexes, so that out of them it is impossible to extract
masculine and feminine sperms, for such cannot be
extracted but from bodies that are male or female,

which metals are not, for if they were, they would propagate without art, God having so ordained it. It is
plain then, that metals (being not male and female)
breed within themselves no seed, and by consequence
cannot give which they have not ; for the truth is, the
seed whereof they spring, is that general seed of the
elements, namely a certain humidity, which appears
(as Sendivow tells us) in forma aquae pinguis, that is
in the form of a fat water. This water is their seed,
their mother and their female, for of this they were
originally made, and if in this they be again resolved
then the child will attract the mother to it, and convert
her totally to his own nature ; and on the contrary, the
spirit of the mother will multiply the spirit of the child
and exalt it to a perfection more than ordinary. This
is the way, and besides it there is none ; for there is no
water under Heaven, from what bodies soever it be
extracted, that hath in it the multiplying virtue, but
this one water which God hath blessed. And here,
though I seem to speak indifferently of metals, yet do
not I : mind the common, for their spirits have been
mortified in the fire. Take therefore our sulphur which
never touched the fire, and whose whole life is whole in
Him : join this living male to a living female, for in
this (as I have elsewhere intimated) lies all the mystery,
namely in the union of a particular spirit to
the universal, by which means Nature is

*Anima
Magica.* strangely exalted and multiplied. Labour
therefore to unite these two substantially

and thoroughly, and thou canst not miss, if thou knowest the applications ; for suffer me to tell thee a secret ; that the application of actives to passives, I mean the manner of it, is the greatest difficulty in all the art. Farewell reader, and enjoy these my labours which I freely communicate to thee : not I assure thee out of any design, for I seek not my own glory but that of God and thy benefit.

COMMENTS UPON THE TWENTY-SEVENTH PARAGRAPH.

This points out that the only means of multiplying metallic natures is to apply their sulphurous nature to the universal feminine fat water ; the oxide or tincture of a metal if dealt with according to art with a careful adjustment of temperature, may then be treated as a ferment.

But as I have said from the beginning, the author is too vague for us to derive any clue to practical alchemy from his work, and I will content myself by pointing out that the human passions, Pride, Envy, Anger, Sloth, Avarice, Gluttony, Lust, have long been associated with the seven gross metals, and that the oxidised metals may be regarded as symbolic of their saving virtues, Humility, Love, Patience, Fortitude, Compassion, Temperance and Chastity.

The Union of a particular to a universal exalts and multiplies strongly. Here is the final lesson then. Let us recognise that only the merging of our human wills with the Universal Will can result in hastening the day of our perfection. It we labour against the World's Will we shall fail, and our work will vanish from off the face of the earth.

SHORT APPENDIX BY WAY
OF ADMONITION TO THE READER.

———

It was not my intention to add anything unto what has been already written: but when I reflect on those vexations I have endured myself in the pursuit of this science, I begin to think I have not said enough. To be a little more plain, know reader, that whosoever seeks the philosopher's mercury in metals, of what kind soever they be, is already out of the way: for that philosophic mercury so much talked of, is a water, and in metal, water there is none; for the sulphur hath not only congealed it there, but hath withal dried it up. This is evident in common quicksilver and antimony, which of all metalline bodies, are the most crude, and yet as crude as they are, their water is exsiccated by their fire; for if we force them into a fume, that fume settles not to a liquid spirit, but into dried flowers. This made the philosophers seek a more crude mineral whose fume was moist, and would settle into water, as being not yet mastered by the sulphur. Such there was none but the mother of mercury, or the first matter,

G

whereof Nature makes the common mercury, and this also they call quicksilver, and a viscous water, for such it is. In this minera the mercurial vapour was not so dry, but it would settle into water, and with this water, they dissolve the metalline bodies; for the moist fume of this minera reduced the metalline dry fumes, so that both turned into one water, and this called mercury philosophical, and duplicated mercury. In this point I need not say more, and if they be not wilfully blind, here is light enough for our metal-mongers, and especially for those confident roasters of antimony, who over the smoke of that drug dream of mysteries, as if they were transported into a certain capnonancy. For my part I deny not but antimony may be reduced to a mercurial water, though I know not to what purpose, for neither our mercury nor our tincture riseth from it, if Basil Valentine may be believed. True it is, that the philosophers use it, but as a mere instrument that goes off again, and so they use even kitchen fire, but it is not their matter or subject, and much less is it common gold, as some ignorants would have it. There is indeed another antimony, which is our sulphur, and the subject of the whole art ; but this is so hard to find, and when it is found, so hard to prepare, that it had almost cast me into despair. How-soever if thou dost seriously consider what I have written, and what hath fallen from me in some places with as much purpose as caution, then verily neither the thing itself not the preparation of it can be hid from thee. To make an end, know that the philosophers have two mercuries or waters, the first and second, their first is the spirit of our antimony and here understand me rightly; their second is that of mercury and Venus philosophical, and this of itself is all sufficient; but to shorten time, the philosophers ferment it with common gold. I have now spoken more than discretion can well allow of, but the sense of those difficulties I have met withal, have carried me thus far. Howsoever be thou cautious in thy construction, lest the name of antimony deceive thee, for so thou mayest run into a fruitless expense of time and substance. This is all I have to say, and now what use to make of it is in thy power; if thou canst believe, it is well; if not, forbear from this art altogether, or thou wilt live to punish thy own incredulity.

COMMENTS UPON THE APPENDIX.

I will end as I began by saying, I have read many Alchemical Treatises, but never one of less use to the practical Alchemist, than this. At the same time I have come across few occult works that have helped me more in my search for the secrets of these Great Adepts—who are the Masters of our Race.

S. S. D. D.

———

" Alas, Alas, that all men should possess the Master-soul, be one with the World-soul, and that possessing it, the Master-soul should so little avail them."

The Book of Golden Precepts.

FINIS.

9 781108 044226